The Cybersecurity Playbook: From Research to Industry Success

The Ultimate Guide to Turning Cybersecurity Knowledge into a Thriving Career, Business, or Brand

Prof. (Dr.) Mohuya Chakraborty

April 2025

Contents

About The Author

Mohuya Chakraborty presently holds the post of Director, of the Cybersecurity Centre of Excellence (CCoE), Dean of faculty Welfare and HRDC, and Professor of the Department of Computer Science and Engineering, University of Engineering & Management (UEM), Kolkata. Before this, she held the position of head of the department of CSE and IT for a tenure of 13 years. She has done B. Tech and M. Tech from the Institute of Radio Physics and Electronics, Calcutta University in the years 1994 and 2000 respectively, and PhD (Engg.) in the field of Mobile Computing from Jadavpur University in 2007. She has a Chartered Management Institute (CMI Level 5) certification in Leadership and Management from Dudley College, London, UK, 2019. She is the topper of M. Tech and subsequently received the prestigious Paresh Lal Dhar Bhowmik Award from Calcutta University. She was also the recipient of the Rashtriya Gaurav Award in 2019. She has been awarded Certification of Appreciation as one of the Top 50 Distinguished HODs CSE/ IT Department in Higher Education Across India for the year 2019 by the Academic Council of uLektz in July 2020. She is a Certified Publons Academy Mentor. She is a member of the editorial board of several international journals. She has published 4 patents and over 100 research papers in reputed international journals and conferences. She is the editor of the book entitled "The Essence of Network Security: An End-To-End Panorama" published by Springer in August 2020 in the series *"Lecture Notes in Networks and Systems"*. She is the volume editor of the Contributed Books; "Proceedings of International Ethical Hacking Conferences (eHaCON-2018, eHaCON-2019, and eHaCON-2024)", in the Springer series *"Advances in Intelligent Systems and Computing book series (AISC volume 811)"*, published by Springer. Dr. Chakraborty is the reviewer of the European Journal of Information Security, Taylor & Francis, and has recently acted as associate editor of the same. Dr. Chakraborty participated in many international conferences as an Organizer, General Chair, Session Chair, and member in Steering, Advisory or International Program Committees. She has handled many research projects worth INR 35 Lakhs funded by the DST, AICTE, CSIR, and NRDC, Government of India, and consultancy projects by non-governmental organizations worth INR 15 Lakhs. Dr. Chakraborty has published ~100 papers in high-impact journals, books, book chapters, and conference proceedings. Her research areas include artificial intelligence, blockchain, network security, cognitive radio, brain-computer interface, parallel computing, etc. She is a senior member of IEEE.

Preface

Whether you're a cybersecurity student, a researcher, or an industry professional, this book shows you exactly how to bridge the gap between theory and practice — and build a meaningful, profitable path in one of the world's most in-demand fields.

In this action-packed playbook, you'll learn how to:

- "Navigate the evolving cybersecurity landscape with confidence."
- "Turn academic research into real-world impact and income."
- "Monetize your skills through consulting, freelancing, and productizing your knowledge."
- "Land corporate cybersecurity roles — even without traditional experience."
- "Build your personal brand, network globally, and launch your own cybersecurity business."

Whether you're eyeing a top-tier job, a thriving side hustle, or launching a startup, this book gives you the tools, strategies, and insider insights to succeed in cybersecurity today — and tomorrow.

No fluff. No theory. Just real strategies from someone who's done it.

Ready to unlock your cybersecurity career potential? Start reading now.

Introduction

Bridging Research, Cybersecurity, and Industry: A New Pathway

Hey there! If you're reading this, chances are you have a passion for cybersecurity, research, or technology and are looking for ways to make a meaningful impact. Maybe you're tired of being stuck in a rigid job that doesn't allow you to innovate, or you've realized that academia moves too slowly to keep up with real-world cyber threats. Maybe you want to monetize your skills, break free from traditional career paths, and create a career that's both financially rewarding and fulfilling.

If that sounds like you, welcome! The goal of this book is to assist you in navigating and utilising your knowledge of artificial intelligence, cybersecurity, and emerging technologies to open doors outside of the conventional academic or business framework. This book will act as your road map whether you're an independent researcher trying to work with industry, a cybersecurity specialist hoping to establish a personal brand, or an entrepreneur hoping to create a long-lasting company.

Why I Wrote This Book

I've witnessed highly skilled cybersecurity workers over the years struggle to land jobs that fully utilise their abilities. Some of them worked on ground-breaking research for years, only to have it published in a publication with minimal practical application. Others held well-paying corporate positions that inhibited their ability to be creative and innovative.

Then there were the driven independent contractors who hustled from job to job, uncertain of how to turn their expertise into a sustainable business.

There must be a better way, I knew.

In order to help people like you escape the constraints of conventional career pathways and investigate fresh, fascinating prospects in cybersecurity, I wrote this book. You can develop a hybrid career that enables you to conduct meaningful work, achieve financial independence, and keep ahead of industry changes instead of having to pick between freelancing, corporate work, or academia. This is your manual for achieving that.

The Problem with Traditional Career Paths in Cybersecurity and Research

For decades, professionals in cybersecurity and research have followed a well-trodden path that, while reliable, often comes with significant limitations. This conventional path usually entails earning a degree, working in business or academic settings, and moving up the corporate or academic ladder. Although this route has led to many prosperous jobs, it is coming under growing criticism for being inflexible, ineffective, and unable to change with the quickly evolving fields of research and technology. I'll go into more detail about each of these phases and the difficulties they pose below.

♣ **Get a Degree: The Time and Financial Investment** - Traditional research and cybersecurity employment routes frequently call for a high level of formal education. Although a bachelor's degree is usually the bare minimum, many professionals go on to earn master's, doctoral, or speciality certificates. This may include attending school for four to ten years (or longer) before even starting a job. Higher education has a substantial financial cost. The opportunity cost of not having a full-time job during this time is significant, and student loan repayment might take years or even decades. The rate of technological advancement frequently surpasses the capacity of educational establishments to revise their curricula. Graduates might thus be forced to master antiquated theories or techniques that have no practical application. Certifications such as CISSP, CEH, or CompTIA Security+ are frequently seen as crucial in the field of cybersecurity. The sheer volume of certifications available, however, can be daunting, and the expense of earning and keeping them increases the financial strain. ♣ **Work in Academia or Corporate: Limited Options -** The pressure to publish research papers is enormous in academic world. Researchers frequently emphasis on subjects that are more likely to get published rather than those that have real-world influence or align with their passions. Academic researchers often face budget constraints, limited access to cutting-edge tools, and bureaucratic hurdles that can stifle innovation. Tenure is a very competitive and frequently political process. Job stability is not guaranteed, even after years of arduous work. Conversely, corporate settings are frequently hierarchical, with strict job descriptions and little room for original problem-solving techniques. Workers might not feel like innovators, but rather like cogs in a machine. Protecting the company's bottom line frequently takes precedence over developing the field or tackling more significant societal issues in corporate cybersecurity roles. Frustration and disengagement may result from corporate professionals' limited control over their projects or the course of their job. ♣ **Climb the Corporate or Academic Ladder: The Slow Grind** - Promotions are frequently determined by seniority rather than merit in both academic and professional contexts. For highly qualified people who are prepared to assume greater responsibility, this can result in a sluggish and discouraging professional advancement. It can be very taxing to navigate the bureaucracy of large organisations. Professionals frequently discover that they are spending more time on administrative duties than on worthwhile work, whether this is due to company red tape or university committees. Innovation and risk-taking are frequently discouraged by traditional professional routes. In order to obtain funding or tenure, academic researchers may limit themselves to "safe" subjects. Employees may be reluctant to make daring suggestions in business settings for fear of upsetting the status quo. Long hours, high levels of stress, and a poor work-life balance might result from the push to go up the corporate ladder. This is particularly accurate in cybersecurity, where the threat landscape is continually growing, and specialists are anticipated to be on call 24/7. ♣ **The Changing Landscape: Why Traditional Paths Are Becoming Obsolete** - In domains like research and cybersecurity, the rate of technological advancement is quickening. Conventional job routes are finding it difficult to stay up due to their slow advancement and concentration on extensive education. Self-directed learning, online courses, and boot camps are all growing in popularity. These choices provide a quicker, more adaptable, and frequently less expensive means of acquiring the abilities required for a prosperous profession. Instead of following traditional career routes, more people are choosing to work as freelancers or launch their own businesses. More freedom, innovation, and the possibility of greater rewards are made possible by this. Professionals can now collaborate with companies worldwide, escaping the limitations of regional labour markets, thanks to the growth of remote work.

The Need for a New Approach

Continuous learning is crucial in a field that is evolving quickly. To remain current, professionals must adopt a lifelong learning mentality and update their knowledge and abilities on a regular basis. There are now more options than the conventional linear professional path. Alternative career routes that offer more freedom and creative chances, such freelancing, entrepreneurship, or working with startups, should be investigated by professionals. Professionals should concentrate on having a significant effect in their sector rather than moving up the corporate or academic ladder. This could entail working on cutting-edge studies, creating original answers to practical issues, or coaching the upcoming generation of experts. Achieving a good work-life balance is essential for wellbeing and long-term success. Professionals should look for positions and companies that value flexibility and employee well-being.

Rethinking Career Paths in Cybersecurity and Research

Many people have found success with the conventional career routes in research and cybersecurity, but they are no longer the only or even the best choice. Professionals in various domains must reconsider how they approach career growth as the globe grows increasingly interconnected and technology advances. They can create successful and rewarding jobs that are more appropriate for the opportunities and difficulties of the twenty-first century by embracing lifelong learning, investigating alternate career options, and concentrating on impact. Although this was effective in the past, these conventional methods are unable to keep up with the rapid changes in the cybersecurity scene today. Let's dissect some of the most significant obstacles.

♣ **Slow Academic Cycles -** There are many bright minds working on significant cybersecurity research in the academic community. The issue is that it can take years for an article to get published, and by then, things might have changed. Threat actors take advantage of vulnerabilities immediately rather than waiting for peer assessments. Your research soon loses relevance if it isn't put to use. It's also well known that academia adopts new trends slowly. Despite the rapid advancement of emerging technologies like blockchain, AI-driven security, and quantum computing, many universities continue to teach antiquated security paradigms. You must leave the academic bubble if you want to be on the cutting edge. ♣ **Corporate Limitations -** Even though many cybersecurity experts find well-paying positions at big businesses, they may not be completely content. Businesses frequently assign experts to highly specialised positions, which restricts their ability to investigate additional cybersecurity topics. Years may pass as a penetration tester performs the same routine evaluations. Instead of creating proactive plans, a security analyst could become mired in a loop of reacting to incidents. Rigid procedures frequently trump creativity, and bureaucracy can impede genuine innovation. ♣ **Financial Constraints -** Even though some cybersecurity positions are lucrative, many experts discover that their salary isn't commensurate with their actual worth. Because they set their own prices and operate on their own terms, independent consultants and business owners frequently make far more money than their corporate counterparts. Think about this: in a corporate position, a penetration testing specialist could make $120,000 year. However, that same specialist may charge $500 per hour as an independent consultant and earn a lot more money with less hours. You don't have to accept a defined pay if you possess specialised knowledge. You can generate several revenue streams, such as product development, content production, and consultancy. ♣

Bureaucratic Constraints - Large organisations have a lot of rules. Dealing with multiple levels of approvals and antiquated procedures can be discouraging for creative thinkers. Do you want to put a new security framework into place? Before you see any results, months may pass between meetings, compliance assessments, and internal politics. Working in these bureaucratic systems can feel like an uphill battle if you're the type of person who thrives on speedy execution. The good news? There are methods to get around these restrictions and pursue a career in cybersecurity at your own pace.

The Rise of the Cybersecurity Entrepreneur

So, what's the alternative? A growing number of professionals are opting to abandon conventional career routes and adopt a new style of working that combines industry, entrepreneurship, and academics. This change is a necessary progression rather than merely a fad.

Here are some reasons why entrepreneurship in cybersecurity is growing.:

♣ **You Make an Immediate Impact** - You may use your knowledge to solve problems in the real world right now, without having to wait for corporate red tape or academic permission. You may begin changing things right now by providing security training, assisting companies in strengthening their defences, or participating in open-source initiatives. ♣ **You Control Your Income -** Don't worry about salary caps. You choose your own prices and earning potential when you work for yourself. There are numerous methods to make money out of your cybersecurity knowledge, such as charging for consultations, starting an online course, or producing a paid newsletter. ♣ **You Go Global -** You're not restricted by geography anymore because of the internet. You can cooperate on worldwide projects, work with clients from any location, and access foreign marketplaces. There are opportunities everywhere, and cybersecurity is a global concern. ♣ **You Design Your Lifestyle -** Want to work from home? Travel while consulting? Set your hours? Taking charge of your career allows you to create a lifestyle that aligns with both your personal and professional objectives. No more strict timetables or pointless meetings—just you, your abilities, and the flexibility to work however you choose.

Organization of the Book

The book is divided into three parts. After the introduction, Part I deals with the evolution of cybersecurity covering five chapters. Part II presents cybersecurity opportunities covered in four chapters. Part III highlights cybersecurity networking and has three chapters. The book concludes with The Cybersecurity Mastery Manifesto.

How This Book Will Help You

This book serves as your road map for overcoming conventional employment limitations and establishing a cybersecurity profession that suits your objectives. You'll learn:

- How to go from corporate work or university to independent consultancy.
- How to generate numerous revenue streams by using your expertise in cybersecurity.
- How to use thought leadership and personal branding to draw in opportunities.
- How to connect with the appropriate individuals and create a global network.
- How to maintain an advantage in a field that is changing quickly.

I'm excited to take you on this journey. Whether you're looking to start small with a side hustle or go all-in on cybersecurity entrepreneurship, this book will give you the strategies and tools to succeed.

So, are you ready to redefine your cybersecurity career and take control of your future? Let's dive in!

Part I   Evolution of Cybersecurity

Chapter 1: The Cybersecurity Industry Landscape

Greetings from the volatile, high-stakes realm of cybersecurity, where the only thing that is constant is change and digital conflicts are waged every second. You have come to the correct site if you have ever wondered how hackers infiltrate multibillion-dollar corporations, how governments engage in cyberwarfare, or how one might make a successful career in this field.

Antivirus software and firewalls are no longer the only components of cybersecurity. The nation-state players, underground illicit marketplaces, and AI-powered cyberthreats in this billion-dollar sector are changing more quickly than most organisations can keep up. This chapter will explore the development of cybersecurity, analyse real-world attacks that altered the course of events, and break down key industry trends. Let's get started, so grab your coffee or energy drink.

1.1 Evolution of Cybersecurity: From Nerds in Basements to Global Warfare

Let's rewind to the late 80s. Back then, cybersecurity wasn't even a thing. The internet was mostly a playground for researchers, and hackers were just curious nerds testing the limits of technology. Fast forward to today, and cybercrime is a trillion-dollar industry with its own economy. Here's how we got here:

The Morris Worm (1988): The First Major Wake-Up Call

The Morris Worm was released in 1988 by Robert Tappan Morris, a 23-year-old Cornell student. Although it was intended to be a scholarly experiment, it ended up erasing roughly 10% of the internet, which was substantial at the time but not very much. The first Computer Emergency Response Team (CERT), which is essentially the SWAT team for digital threats, was established as a result of the turmoil.

Stuxnet (2010): When Cyber Attacks Went Nuclear

Next came Stuxnet. This cyberattack wasn't your typical one. This worm, which was allegedly created by the United States and Israel, was designed to particularly target Iran's nuclear centrifuges in order to undermine its nuclear program. It was the first attack of its kind—a weapon that could destroy the real world without firing a single shot. Suddenly, cybersecurity was about cyberwarfare and national security, not just data protection.

The Equifax Breach (2017): The Attack That Exposed 147 Million People

Let's fast-forward to 2017. Hackers were able to obtain 147 million people's personal information, including financial information and Social Security numbers, due to an Apache Struts vulnerability. This hack demonstrated the value of patch maintenance and the vulnerability of even big businesses to straightforward vulnerabilities.

The SolarWinds Attack (2020): The Supply Chain Nightmare

The SolarWinds hack was one of the most advanced supply chain attacks in recent memory, compromising thousands of organisations, including government institutions in the United States. By inserting malware within a trusted software update, hackers were able to snoop on victims for months. The necessity of zero-trust security models and ongoing attention to detail was reaffirmed by this attack.

1.2 The Biggest Trends Shaping Cybersecurity Today

After discussing the past, let's discuss the future of cybersecurity. Innovation in the sector is booming, but so are the risks. The following are the main trends that are defining the cybersecurity environment:

AI-Powered Cybersecurity: The New Arms Race

The concept of artificial intelligence (AI) has two sides. On the one hand, by instantly analysing vast volumes of data, it enables organisations to identify dangers more quickly. However, hackers are also leveraging AI to deepfake phishing scams, automate attacks, and even anticipate security flaws before businesses can. You cannot afford to ignore AI if you work in cybersecurity.

The Rise of Zero Trust Architecture

Do you recall when networks were thought of as castles with moats? Those times are over. Businesses nowadays are adopting a "zero-trust" strategy, which makes the assumption that attacks might originate from anywhere, including within the network. This entails constant identification, stringent access restrictions, and never putting your blind faith in any individual or gadget.

Ransomware-as-a-Service (RaaS): Yes, It's a Thing

Ransomware has evolved into a legitimate economic strategy for cybercriminals. Even non-professional hackers may rent pre-made ransomware kits and launch attacks with no technical expertise thanks to Ransomware-as-a-Service (RaaS). Hospitals, towns, and large enterprises have all been the target of these attacks, which have increased dramatically. In order to recover their data, many organisations have had to pay millions of dollars in ransom.

Regulatory Crackdowns: Governments Are Waking Up

Governments are taking action after years of breaches that exposed the personal information of millions of individuals. Companies are being forced to treat data privacy seriously by laws like the California Consumer Privacy Act (CCPA) and the General Data privacy Regulation (GDPR) in Europe. If you work with data, you must be aware of compliance regulations or face steep penalties.

1.3 Case Study: The Colonial Pipeline Ransomware Attack (2021): A Wake-Up Call

Imagine seeing kilometres of automobiles lining up at petrol stations when you wake up one morning. People are worried, storing fuel, and prices are skyrocketing. When the Colonial Pipeline, one of the biggest petroleum providers in the United States, came to a grinding halt in May 2021, it wasn't a scenario from a dystopian film; it was real.

The offender? Colonial Pipeline was forced to cease operations due to a severe ransomware attack by a group of cybercriminals known as DarkSide. Gas shortages, public fear, and a multi-million-dollar disaster were the immediate and severe repercussions, since its 5,500-mile pipeline supplied about half of the gasoline used on the East Coast.

How did the hackers manage to do that, then? Unbelievably, they gained access by using a single hacked VPN password. Only a weak link in the security chain—no Hollywood-style heist, no sophisticated hacking. Even worse, the VPN did not have multi-factor authentication (MFA) configured, which meant that the attackers would have the kingdom's keys once they figured out the password.

Once inside, the ransomware quickly spread, encrypting Colonial Pipeline's vital systems and forcing the business to choose between paying the ransom and suffering extended outages. Colonial had to make a difficult decision under extreme pressure: they sent the hackers $4.4 million in Bitcoin in return for a decryption key. Even so, the harm had already been done, and the recovery was sluggish. The vulnerability of key infrastructure was made clear by the attack.

However, the story didn't stop there. A portion of the ransom was ultimately traced down and collected by U.S. law enforcement, delivering a clear warning that cybercriminals would not always get away with it. The true lesson, however, was obvious: this catastrophe could have been avoided.

Lessons Learned from Colonial Pipeline's Mistake: A Deep Dive into Cybersecurity Failures and Solutions

A turning point in the history of cybersecurity was the May 2021 Colonial Pipeline ransomware attack. It revealed the wide-ranging effects of poor security procedures in addition to the weaknesses of vital infrastructure. What could happen to companies, countries, and even individuals if a single hacked password could bring down a major energy supplier? The attack brought to light an important reality: cybersecurity is becoming more than just an IT problem; it is a question of national security, company survival, and societal resilience. Here is a more thorough examination of the lessons Colonial Pipeline learnt from its errors and how they relate to the larger cybersecurity environment.

- **Multi-Factor Authentication (MFA) is Non-Negotiable**

A single-password-protected VPN account that had been compromised was used to launch the Colonial Pipeline attack. Hackers were able to infiltrate the company's network and spread ransomware because of this one point of failure. By forcing users to submit two or more kinds of verification before gaining access to a system, multi-factor authentication

(MFA) offers an additional layer of protection. For instance, a hacker would still require a biometric scan or a one-time code delivered to a trusted device in order to obtain access, even if they were to acquire a password. The risk of unwanted access is greatly decreased by MFA. Microsoft claims that MFA is capable of thwarting 99.9% of account compromise attempts. MFA is a low-cost, high-impact solution that can help firms avoid disastrous breaches. The Colonial Pipeline incident serves as a clear reminder that passwords are no longer enough. To safeguard sensitive systems and data, MFA must be implemented as a routine procedure by organisations, governments, and individuals.

- **Network Segmentation is Critical**

Colonial Pipeline's IT network was too closely linked to its operational technology (OT), which controls the flow of petroleum. Operations were completely shut down as a result of the OT systems being impacted by the penetration of the IT network. To prevent malware from spreading or unauthorised access, a network might be segmented into smaller, isolated parts. Businesses may limit harm and contain breaches by separating vital systems, such as OT, from regular IT networks. The repercussions of a breach can be disastrous in essential infrastructure areas including transportation, healthcare, and energy. Segmentation guarantees that the system will continue to function even if one area of the network is compromised. The attack on the Colonial Pipeline emphasises the necessity of a "zero trust" architecture, in which no component of the network is intrinsically reliable. Companies need to build their networks with the assumption that breaches will occur.

- **Incident Response Plans Save Time and Money**

Colonial Pipeline was unable to contain the breach and recover from the attack in a timely manner because they lacked a well-practiced incident response plan. Their decision to pay the ransom was probably influenced by this lack of readiness. The actions that a company should do in the case of a cyberattack are described in an efficient incident response plan. This entails locating the breach, minimising the harm, eliminating the danger, and resuming business activities. Frequent simulations and drills guarantee that teams are ready to respond swiftly and decisively. In the event of a cyberattack, time is critical. The difference between a small disturbance and a major disaster can be determined by how successfully a response plan is implemented. A quicker reaction might have saved Colonial Pipeline from having to stop operations and pay the ransom. The incident emphasises how crucial preventative cybersecurity measures are. Businesses need to make investments in incident response skills, such as crisis management, forensic investigation, and threat identification.

- **Paying the Ransom is Not a Solution**

Colonial Pipeline hoped to swiftly restore operations by paying the hackers a ransom of $4.4 million. Despite being reasonable in the circumstances, this ruling established a risky precedent. Ransom payments encourage more attacks and support criminal organisations. Additionally, there is no assurance that payment would lead to the recovery of systems or data. Hackers occasionally refuse to give the decryption keys or demand more money. The best defence against ransomware is a solid backup and disaster recovery plan. Organisations can recover operations without caving in to hacker demands by routinely backing up and securely storing data. The attack on the Colonial Pipeline brings to light the moral and practical quandaries surrounding ransom payments. Although it could appear to be a short-term solution, it compromises long-term security and feeds the cycle of cybercrime. Bans on ransom payments are becoming more and more popular among governments and business associations. Instead of depending on reactive tactics, organisations should prioritise prevention and resilience.

- **Cybersecurity is Everyone's Responsibility**

For governments, corporations, and citizens alike, the Colonial Pipeline attack served as a wake-up call. It proved that cybersecurity is a crucial business function that demands attention from stakeholders, employees, and leadership, and that it is not solely the domain of IT departments. To safeguard their companies, executives and board members need to give cybersecurity top priority and set aside the required funds. This covers spending on talent, training, and technology. One of the main reasons for cyber incidents is human mistake. Employees that participate in regular training and awareness programs are better able to identify phishing attempts, create secure passwords, and adhere to security best practices. The need for cooperation between the public and private sectors was brought to light by the Colonial Pipeline attack. To exchange threat intelligence, create best practices, and bolster defences, governments, corporations, and cybersecurity specialists must collaborate.

- **The Growing Demand for Cybersecurity Professionals**

The attack on the Colonial Pipeline made clear how urgently qualified cybersecurity specialists are needed. The need for professionals who can develop, execute, and oversee security measures has never been greater due to the sophistication of cyberthreats. Jobs like incident responders, threat analysts, security architects, and compliance specialists are in high demand as a result of the attack. The options for people who want to pursue a career in cybersecurity are numerous and diverse. To address complex difficulties, the cybersecurity sector requires a variety of viewpoints and skill sets. This encompasses not only technical proficiency but also communication, risk management, and strategic planning abilities. A reminder that cybersecurity is a dynamic and constantly changing industry is provided by the Colonial Pipeline attack. Professionals must promise incessant learning and adaptation to stay ahead of evolving threats.

Turning Lessons into Action

The attack on the Colonial Pipeline taught us the value of cybersecurity in a difficult but essential way. It made clear the dangers of insufficient security procedures, the weaknesses of vital infrastructure, and the pressing need for preventative action. The attack is a clear warning to people, companies, and governments that cybersecurity is crucial and not a choice.

Organisations can drastically lower their chance of becoming victims of cyberattacks by installing multi-factor authentication, segmenting their networks, creating incident response procedures, and refraining from paying ransom. However, the increasing need for cybersecurity specialists offers people the chance to pursue fulfilling professions in an area vital to the development of our digital world.

Colonial Pipeline made a mistake, but the lessons learnt are clear: cybersecurity is a shared responsibility, and now is the time to take action. Whether you're a government official, corporate executive, or aspiring cybersecurity specialist, the decisions you make now will determine our ability to withstand threats in the future.

The Hottest Cybersecurity Skills in 2024

Companies are rushing to acquire experts who can safeguard their networks, identify dangers, and stop the next major breach because cyber threats are changing more quickly than ever before. These are the things you should concentrate on if you want to succeed in cybersecurity:

Cloud Security & DevSecOps: The Future of Protection: Securing platforms like AWS, Azure, and Google Cloud is crucial as more and more enterprises move their operations to the cloud. You may become a highly sought-after expert by learning how to use technologies like Terraform and Ansible, implement Infrastructure as Code (IaC) security, and lock down cloud infrastructures.

AI & Threat Intelligence: Beating Hackers at Their Own Game: AI is being used by increasingly intelligent cybercriminals to automate attacks. Security professionals must become experts in threat hunting, cybersecurity machine learning, and SIEM solutions like Splunk, QRadar, and Elastic Security if they want to stay ahead of the curve. Gaining an understanding of the MITRE ATT&CK Framework can also help you monitor and prevent assaults before they become more serious.

Ethical Hacking & Red Teaming: Think Like a Hacker: If you love the thrill of outsmarting cybercriminals, ethical hacking might be your calling. Learning how to break into systems legally using tools like Burp Suite, Metasploit, and Kali Linux can open doors to exciting careers in penetration testing and red teaming. And if you're feeling adventurous, bug bounty programs let you turn hacking skills into real cash.

Compliance & Risk Management: The Backbone of Cybersecurity: Cybersecurity isn't just about stopping hackers—it's also about following regulations. With privacy laws like GDPR, CCPA, and HIPAA, companies need experts who can conduct security audits, create policies, and ensure compliance with NIST and ISO frameworks. If you have a knack for strategy and policy, this field offers steady, well-paying opportunities.

1.4 Final Thoughts

The field of cybersecurity presents both opportunities and challenges. The options are unlimited, whether your goal is to build a cybersecurity firm, get a six-figure career, or assist in defending businesses from online attacks. Continue to learn, be inquisitive, and never undervalue the might of a well-planned cyberattack or the experts who prevent it.

Chapter 2: Cracking the Code: Turning Cybersecurity Research into Industry Gold

You have worked in academics for years, researching cybersecurity extensively, identifying weaknesses, creating attack models, and possibly even publishing a few papers in prestigious publications. The worst part, though, is that the industry isn't exactly hammering down your door. Why? Because research that remains confined to academic circles is like a state-of-the-art vault without a key—impressive, but ultimately inaccessible—in the rapidly evolving field of cybersecurity.

The reality is that many bright brains in cybersecurity find it difficult to make the leap from research labs to practical impact. However, individuals who figure out how to close the gap—those who crack the code—end up working on cutting-edge technology, influencing international security standards, and, let's face it, earning a lot of money. The goal of this chapter is to assist you in doing so.

2.1 Why Academia Falls Short in Cybersecurity?

Let's face it, while academia excels at producing knowledge, it frequently finds it difficult to use that knowledge in practical ways. For a very long time, academia has been a vital component of knowledge generation, encouraging creativity and expanding human comprehension. However, the academic community frequently finds it difficult to convert its theoretical advances into workable, real-world cybersecurity solutions. Universities and research facilities are excellent at coming up with concepts and carrying out trials in controlled settings, but they usually fall short when it comes to solving the pressing, rapidly evolving cybersecurity concerns. The main causes of academia's frequent inability to satisfy the needs of the cybersecurity sector will be discussed below, along with solutions.

The biggest issue?

- **Too Much Theory, Not Enough Action**

The Academic Focus: The search for theoretical knowledge, not real-world application, is frequently the driving force behind academic study. In order to validate ideas, create models, and publish papers, researchers frequently work in extremely controlled settings that don't accurately represent the disorderly, unpredictable character of actual cyberthreats.

The Speed of Cyber Threats: The speed at which cybercriminals work is astounding, and their tactics, methods, and procedures (TTPs) are always changing. An academic study may already be outdated by the time it is planned, carried out, reviewed by peers, and published. Much of the research is useless for practitioners because of the gap between the speed of cyber threats and academia.

The Gap Between Theory and Practice: Even though scholarly research might yield sophisticated solutions; these solutions frequently overlook the complexity of real-world systems. For instance, due to compatibility problems or performance limitations, a theoretical encryption method may be mathematically valid but impossible to use in a large-scale commercial setting.

- **Research in Isolation: The Silo Problem**

Lack of Collaboration: Academic researchers frequently operate alone, cut off from the businesses and institutions that regularly deal with cyberthreats. Because of this lack of cooperation, researchers might not completely comprehend the difficulties faced by cybersecurity experts, which could result in solutions that are out of step with practical requirements.

Industry Expertise: Experts in cybersecurity have direct knowledge of new dangers and the resources required to counter them. Academic research runs the risk of being out of date or irrelevant if these practitioners don't contribute.

The Publication Trap: Rather than the research's usefulness, academic success is frequently determined by the quantity of papers published and citations obtained. This gives researchers a distorted incentive to value quantity over quality and theoretical rigour above practicality.

- **Funding and Resource Constraints**

Limited Resources: Universities and other research organisations frequently lack the resources and facilities required to conduct large-scale cybersecurity solution testing. Even if a researcher creates a promising new security tool, they might not have the resources necessary to evaluate it under stress in an enterprise-level, realistic setting.

High-Pressure Scenarios: The severe strain of real-world attacks, which frequently entail highly skilled adversaries and dire repercussions, must be tolerated by cybersecurity systems. Academic research may yield theoretically good but practically worthless solutions if these conditions cannot be replicated.

Funding Priorities: The most urgent cybersecurity issues might not be met by academic financing, which is frequently linked to particular study fields or governmental agendas. Researchers might therefore be compelled to work on issues that are less pertinent to business requirements.

- **The Accessibility Problem**

Buried in Journals: Even in cases where scholarly research yields novel insights, these discoveries are frequently published in specialised publications that are closed to the general cybersecurity community.

Industry experts find it challenging to obtain the most recent research because many of these journals are protected by paywalls.

Language Barrier: Non-academics may find it challenging to comprehend academic articles because they are usually written in complex, technical jargon. This hinders the flow of knowledge from academia to industry by erecting a barrier between academics and practitioners.

Lack of Dissemination: Scholarly organisations frequently struggle to properly communicate their findings to the general public. Even the most significant research might be overlooked and underutilised if there isn't a deliberate attempt to share findings with industry stakeholders.

- **The Real-World Impact Gap**

Measuring Success: Academic metrics like citations, h-index, and journal impact factors are frequently used to gauge achievement in the academic world. However, the impact of the research in the real world is not reflected in these measurements. While a less-known study might provide a revolutionary answer to a critical cybersecurity issue, a highly referenced paper might have little to no real-world relevance.

Industry Priorities: Effective, scalable, and simple-to-implement solutions are given top priority in the cybersecurity sector. Conversely, academic research frequently places a higher value on theoretical contributions and innovation. Even the most creative academic research may not be able to make inroads in the market due to this imbalance.

- **Bridging the Gap: How to Fix Academia's Shortcomings**

Foster Collaboration: Universities should aggressively pursue collaborations with cybersecurity companies, governmental organisations, and other stakeholders in order to bridge the gap between academics and industry. Collaborative research initiatives can guarantee that scholarly work is informed by industrial knowledge and rooted in real-world problems.

Focus on Practical Impact: Academic institutions ought to give more attention to how research may be applied in the real world and reward academics who come up with solutions to pressing issues. This can entail developing new success criteria that give usability and applicability first priority.

Improve Accessibility: Academic institutions ought to work hard to disseminate their findings to the larger cybersecurity community. This could entail disseminating open-access research, organising conferences with an industry focus, and converting scholarly discoveries into practical advice for practitioners.

Invest in Real-World Testing: In order to test their findings in real-world, high-pressure settings, academic institutions should look for financing and collaborations. This can entail working with business partners to carry out extensive pilot projects or simulations.

Encourage Interdisciplinary Research: The topic of cybersecurity is multidisciplinary and calls for knowledge of computer science, psychology, law, and other fields. In order to create comprehensive solutions that cover the technical, human, and legal facets of cybersecurity, universities should support interdisciplinary research.

Rethinking Academia's Role in Cybersecurity

Even though academics has significantly advanced the topic of cybersecurity, the urgent, fast-paced problems of the actual world are frequently too big for its typical methodology to handle. Universities run the risk of losing their relevance in the battle against cyber risks if they operate in silos, prioritise academic metrics above real-world applications, and place an excessive amount of emphasis on theory.

In order to close this gap, academia needs to reconsider its goals and adopt a more accessible, pragmatic, and cooperative research methodology. Academic institutions may play a critical role in creating the creative, practical solutions required to safeguard our digital future by collaborating closely with industry stakeholders, emphasising real-world impact, and disseminating their findings to the larger community. Now is the moment to take action, and the stakes are high. Cybersecurity is an issue of global security and resilience, not merely an academic exercise.

Breaking Out of the Research Bubble

[Scene: A cybersecurity conference, coffee break area. Harry, a cybersecurity researcher, and Jordan, an industry consultant, are discussing career transitions.]

Harry: *[sipping coffee]* You know, sometimes I feel like all my research is just… collecting dust. I mean, I publish papers, present at conferences, but what's the impact? It's frustrating.

Jordan: *[nodding]* I get it. Academic research is crucial, but if it never reaches the industry, it's like having a cure for a disease and locking it in a lab.

Harry: That's exactly it! I spend months working on cutting-edge threat detection models, but companies are still using outdated security measures.

Jordan: So why not bring your research into the real world? MITRE did it with ATT&CK, and look where that got them—global adoption.

Harry: MITRE had backing. A big name. I'm just one researcher.

Jordan: That's where most researchers get stuck. They think they need a massive platform. But what they really need is industry engagement. Have you ever talked to cybersecurity firms while working on your research?

Harry: Not really. My focus was getting published.

Jordan: See, that's the problem. Research without real-world testing is like designing a parachute without ever jumping out of a plane. You need to collaborate with security teams, see what works, and refine it.

Harry: That makes sense. But let's say I do that—how do I make a career out of it?

Jordan: There are plenty of ways. Consulting is one. Companies are dying for experts who can translate research into practical security solutions. You could also patent your work or license it to cybersecurity vendors.

Harry: *[raising an eyebrow]* Consulting? I've never thought of myself as a businessperson.

Jordan: You don't have to be. You just need to know how to market your expertise. Start with a niche—maybe AI-driven security or cloud vulnerabilities. Share insights online, write whitepapers, attend industry events. Before you know it, people will be coming to you for advice.

Harry: So, instead of waiting for my research to be noticed, I should actively put it in front of the right people?

Jordan: Exactly. Be your own advocate. No one's going to hand you an industry breakthrough—you have to create it.

Harry: *[grinning]* Alright, Jordan. You've convinced me. Time to take my research out of the lab and into the battlefield.

Jordan: Now you're talking. Welcome to the real world of cybersecurity.

The Research Paper Problem

Have you ever wondered why so many important advances in cybersecurity are never commercialised? The reason for this is that research frequently fails to meet industry demands. Many scholarly ideas are simply unworkable for practical use since they don't mesh effectively with current security systems. Additionally, researchers frequently concentrate only on technical issues, ignoring aspects like ROI, scalability, and compliance—all of which are crucial for businesses wishing to implement new security measures.

These solutions are only theoretical if they are not tested in the actual world. They never get to the security professionals who truly need them if they are not visible outside of academic circles. The outcome? As fraudsters keep coming up with new ideas, brilliant ideas gather dust. However, things don't have to be this way. By changing their perspective and thinking more like entrepreneurs, problem-solvers, and business executives rather than merely scholars, researchers can escape this loop.

2.2 MITRE's ATT&CK Framework: A Case Study in Doing It Right

The nonprofit research group MITRE figured out how to make scholarly research important. As a means of classifying cyber adversary behaviours, they created ATT&CK (Adversarial Tactics, Techniques, and Common Knowledge). What began as an internal research project swiftly evolved into one of the most popular cybersecurity frameworks globally.

These days, ATT&CK is used by security teams worldwide for threat intelligence and detecting, analysing and forecasting cyberattacks. Red teams use ATT&CK's strategies to model actual cyberthreats in order to bolster an organization's defences. In order to enhance detection and response capabilities, security manufacturers have also embraced ATT&CK and incorporated it into their solutions.

So, why did ATT&CK succeed when so many other research projects failed? First, MITRE didn't work in isolation—they collaborated with government agencies, cybersecurity professionals, and private companies to refine the framework. Second, they made ATT&CK open-access and continuously updated it with real-world cyber incidents. It wasn't just a one-time research paper—it was a living, evolving tool that adapted to new threats. Most importantly, ATT&CK was built for practicality. Instead of trying to impress academic journals, MITRE focused on making their framework useful for real-world security teams. And because it was easy to integrate with existing security tools like SIEMs and EDR systems, adoption skyrocketed.

The lesson here? If you want your research to have an impact, don't just aim for citations—aim for usability.

2.3 Monetizing Cybersecurity Research: Turning Knowledge into Cash

Alright, let's cut to the chase: your cybersecurity research doesn't have to gather dust in some academic journal that only five people will ever read. Nope. Your expertise? It's gold. And in a world where cyber threats are growing faster than weeds in an untended garden, businesses are *desperate* for people like you. The best part? You can turn that brainpower of yours into serious cash. Let's break it down—how you can take your research, slap a price tag on it, and start making an impact (and a pay check) in the real world.

- **Consulting: The Fast Track to Cashing In**

If you've got the skills, consulting is your golden ticket. Companies are scrambling to protect themselves from hackers, ransomware, and all the other digital boogeymen out there. And guess what? They're willing to pay top dollar for someone who knows their stuff. Whether it's AI security, malware forensics, or cloud security, your research can be the foundation of a thriving consulting career.

How to Get Started?

What are you *really* good at? Maybe it's zero-trust architecture, or perhaps you're a wizard at penetration testing. Whatever it is, find something businesses actually need. (Hint: they need a lot.) Start publishing industry-friendly content—think whitepapers, blog posts, and case studies. Show the world you're not just an academic; you're a problem-solver. Get out there. Join cybersecurity communities, attend conferences, and rub elbows with industry leaders. The more people know your name, the more opportunities will come your way. Host free workshops or webinars. Give people a taste of what you can do, and they'll come knocking for more. Go solo, join a consulting firm, or start your own gig. Simply make sure you have a strategy in place for monetising your expertise.

- **Patents and Licensing: Protecting Your Genius**

If you've an idea about a revolutionary cybersecurity expertise or system, don't just let it sit in a lab. Protect it. Patent it. License it. Here's where the big money is. Patented technology is highly valued by businesses; it's like candy for investors and startups. Additionally, they will pay to use your idea if it is as good as you believe.

How to Make It Happen?

Don't attempt to handle the patent procedure by yourself. Look for a lawyer with expertise in intellectual property and cybersecurity. They will walk you through the procedure and assist you in determining whether your study is worthy of a patent. Not every research project can be made profitable. Is this something that businesses will use? Does it address an actual issue? You're on the right track if the response is yes. You can go the traditional patent route, which gives you exclusive rights to your invention. Or, if you're feeling generous (and strategic), you can opt for an open-source model with licensing clauses. This way, your tech gets widespread adoption, and you still get paid.

- **Startups and Entrepreneurship: Build It, and They Will Come**

Got a killer idea that could revolutionize cybersecurity? Why not build a company around it? Startups are risky, sure, but they're also where the real magic happens. If your research has the potential to disrupt the industry, investors will be lining up to throw money at you.

How to Get Started?

Before you quit your day job, make sure there's a market for your product. Talk to potential customers, run surveys, and test your idea in the real world. You can't do it all alone. Find co-founders, developers, and marketers who share your vision and complement your skills. Pitch your idea to venture capitalists, angel investors, or even crowdfunding platforms. If your research is as groundbreaking as you think, the money will follow. Start small, prove your concept, and then scale up. The cybersecurity world moves fast, so you'll need to be agile and adaptable.

41

- **Writing and Speaking: Share Your Knowledge (and Get Paid)**

If you've got a knack for explaining complex concepts in a way that doesn't put people to sleep, you can monetize your research through writing and speaking. Cybersecurity is a hot topic, and everyone wants to hear from the experts.

How to Make It Work?

Yes, an actual book. Whether it's a deep dive into your research or a practical guide for businesses, a well-written book can establish you as an authority in the field. Conferences, webinars, and corporate events are always looking for knowledgeable speakers. Charge a fee, and use the opportunity to promote your consulting services or products. Platforms like Udemy, Coursera, and LinkedIn Learning are hungry for cybersecurity content. Package your research into a course, and earn passive income while helping others learn. You may land up with 5000+ learners from 123+ countries speaking 34+ languages like many instructors on Udemy.

- **Partnerships and Collaborations: Team Up for Success**

Sometimes, the best way to monetize your research is to team up with others. Partner with companies, universities, or even government agencies to bring your ideas to life.

How to Make It Happen?

Look for organizations that align with your goals and have the resources to bring your research to market. Whether it's a revenue-sharing agreement, a licensing deal, or a joint venture, make sure you're getting a fair share of the profits. Your partner's connections can open doors you never knew existed. Use them to scale your impact—and your income.

The Bottom Line: Your Research is Worth More Than You Think

Here's the thing: cybersecurity isn't just a field—it's a *movement*. And your research is a slice of that movement. There are several opportunities out there for you, whether you choose to share your knowledge, create a business, consult, or patent. Therefore, don't allow your genius to be confined to academia. Apply it in the real world and begin making money off of your knowledge. After all, ensuring that your research is visible, effective, and profitable is the best strategy to combat cyberthreats. Go out there now and make money like a pro. Your your account and the globe will both appreciate it.

2.4 Final Thoughts: Make Your Research Work for You

Here's your strategy if you're a cybersecurity researcher hoping to have an influence:

Don't wait till your research is published to find out whether firms are interested; get involved with the industry early. Think outside of the classroom; usability is more important for success than citations alone. Don't let worthwhile research go to waste; instead, get money from it through consultancy, patents, or licensing. Keep in touch by participating in debates, joining cybersecurity communities, and ensuring that your work remains current.

Research on cybersecurity has the potential to transform the world, but only if it breaks free from academic boundaries. Innovative thinkers who can go beyond theory and provide practical solutions are needed in the industry. It's time to put your knowledge into action if you possess it.

Chapter 3: Monetizing Cybersecurity Skills Beyond Academia

If you know how to use your skills, cybersecurity is a goldmine, not simply a job. Even if academics offer a strong basis, actual money moves outside of lecture halls. There are countless options whether you work as a penetration tester, security consultant, or security-focused software developer.

This chapter will explore the story of a successful bug bounty hunter, outline three of the most lucrative ways to monetise your cybersecurity expertise, and provide you with a strategy for attracting high-paying clients.

3.1 The 3 Most Profitable Income Streams in Cybersecurity

Do you want to make a lot of money with your cybersecurity expertise? There are many methods to do it, which is good news. There is a path that suits your needs, whether they are for flexibility, high-impact job, or passive income. Let's examine three of the most profitable cybersecurity income streams.

Freelancing: Be Your Own Boss

Imagine choosing which tasks to work on after waking up and getting your coffee. You, your abilities, and the autonomy to determine your own prices—no employer, no strict schedules. That's what makes freelancing so great.

Security specialists are in high demand, yet many businesses are reluctant to commit to full-time staff. Here's where you come in. For services like penetration testing, where ethical hackers reveal flaws before the bad guys do, businesses are willing to pay big bucks. Another treasure trove is security assessments; businesses want experts to examine their infrastructure and suggest enhancements. Incident reaction comes next. Businesses will pay a hefty price for someone who can limit the damage when a hack occurs because they are terrified.

You're in luck if you're concerned about cloud security. As more businesses move to the cloud, they will gladly hire professionals who know how to lock things down because they understand how important it is to secure such settings. Not to mention malware analysis and reverse engineering—having a thorough awareness of cyberthreats makes you a tremendous asset.

So, how do you begin? Show off your abilities first. Create a portfolio to demonstrate your work on intriguing projects, research contributions, and security evaluations. Then, join websites where clients are actively seeking cybersecurity experts, such as Upwork, Fiverr, Bugcrowd, Cobalt, or Toptal. However, don't rely solely on platforms; instead, network extensively. Participate in forums, go to cybersecurity conferences, and establish connections. Opportunities will increase as more people become aware of what you do.

Diversifying your revenue streams is one of the biggest benefits of working as a freelance cybersecurity professional. In contrast to regular employment, freelancing enables you to work on several projects at once, collaborate with clients from diverse industries, and investigate different facets of cybersecurity. For instance, you may combine writing security training materials or offering compliance framework advice with penetration testing jobs. This adaptability guarantees a consistent cash stream even in the event that one project kind slows down, in addition to keeping your work interesting. Furthermore, freelancing enables you to test out various price structures, such hourly rates, project-based fees, or retainer agreements, in order to optimise your profits according to the value you offer.

Developing a strong personal brand is another essential component of becoming a successful freelancer. Making an impression is essential in a crowded market, and your reputation may be your greatest strength. Start by setting up a polished blog or website where you can post case studies, insights, and project success stories. Interact with the cybersecurity community by posting insightful information, taking part in conversations, and making contributions to open-source projects on sites like GitHub, LinkedIn, and Twitter. This exposure will eventually establish you as a thought leader and draw in customers who are prepared to pay more for your knowledge. Keep in mind that successful self-marketing and establishing credibility with potential clients are more important aspects of freelancing than technical proficiency. You may build a successful freelancing career that provides both financial rewards and professional fulfilment by fusing your skills with a strong personal brand.

Consulting: Big Money, Big Impact
Consulting is about taking a backseat and giving firms advice on how to avoid being hacked in the first place, whereas freelancing is about taking on practical jobs. And believe me, businesses are prepared to shell out a lot of cash for it.

All businesses, regardless of size, require assistance with defining security policies, guaranteeing compliance, and managing cybersecurity risks. You can provide consulting services in risk management, compliance audits, and security policy formulation if you are an expert in these fields. Because, let's face it, most security breaches begin with an employee clicking on the incorrect link, businesses also require assistance in teaching their staff. Additionally, if you are skilled at crisis preparation, you may earn a lot of money by assisting companies in being ready for cyberattacks before they occur.

It's not as hard as it seems to get started in consulting. Choosing a speciality, such as cloud security, compliance, or penetration testing, makes you stand out, and certifications like CISSP, CISM, or CEH immediately increase your credibility. Having a clean LinkedIn profile and a website that highlights your experience are essential for a professional online presence. And networking is crucial once more. You will acquire high-paying clients more quickly if you network with more companies at cybersecurity events and online communities.

Staying ahead of new threats and market trends is crucial for cybersecurity consultants to succeed. The field of cybersecurity is always changing as new attack methods, weaknesses, and legal requirements appear on a regular basis. You may provide clients with state-of-the-art solutions that tackle their most urgent issues by remaining educated through ongoing learning, whether through conferences, industry publications, or certifications. Furthermore, utilising tools such as risk assessment frameworks or threat intelligence platforms can improve your consulting offerings by making them more impactful and data-driven. When consultants take the initiative to keep current and provide useful insights, clients are more likely to trust and invest in them.

The development of enduring relationships with your clients is another essential component of successful consulting. Cybersecurity is a continuous process that necessitates frequent evaluations, upgrades, and adjustments. You can get repeat business and retainers by presenting yourself as a reliable collaborator rather than a one-time consultant. To keep your clients' defences robust, provide follow-up services like recurring security assessments, refresher training for staff, or incident response exercises. Furthermore, giving clients concise, useful reports and suggestions at the conclusion of each engagement demonstrates your knowledge and helps them recognise the worth of your work. Satisfied customers will eventually recommend you to others and come back for more services, building a profitable and long-lasting consulting business.

Product Creation: Build Once, Earn Forever

Product development is the best option if you want to earn money in cybersecurity while you sleep. You make something once and sell it repeatedly rather than exchanging your time for cash.

This can be done in a variety of ways. Writing ebooks or developing online courses is one of the simplest; if you are knowledgeable in security analysis, ethical hacking, or compliance best practices, people will pay to learn from you. Creating cybersecurity tools, whether they are commercial or open-source, is an additional approach. Some of the most effective security technologies available were initially side projects created by security experts who recognised an issue and developed a fix.

Consider introducing a SaaS (Software as a Service) security product if you have broader plans. If businesses find value in vulnerability scanners, log monitoring tools, or automation platforms, they can generate recurring revenue. Offering subscription-based security services is another option if you'd rather have a consistent source of income. Businesses like managed security solutions that enable them to outsource their cyber defence.

The secret to monetising a cybersecurity product is straightforward: identify a real issue that businesses or individuals face, then discover a solution. To test your idea with actual people, start with a minimum viable product (MVP). After you've established that it works, concentrate on promotion. Social media, SEO, and cybersecurity forums are excellent venues for audience development. Try out several monetisation strategies, such as enterprise licensing, tiered pricing, or free trials, until you determine which one works best.

Using your knowledge to create specialised solutions is another successful strategy for cybersecurity product development. If your area of expertise is penetration testing, for instance, you could develop a framework or toolkit that makes the process easier for other experts. In a similar vein, if compliance is your strong suit, think about creating automated tools, checklists, or templates that assist companies in complying with laws like GDPR, PCI-DSS, or ISO 27001 requirements. These goods not only address certain problems but also establish you as an expert in your field, which makes it simpler to draw in clients who are prepared to pay for specialised services. Furthermore, providing frequent updates or premium support can guarantee client pleasure while generating a consistent flow of income.

In the process of creating new products, collaboration can also be quite important. You can produce more inventive and reliable items by collaborating with other cybersecurity specialists or developers than you could on your alone. You can combine your abilities and reach a wider audience by, for example, co-developing a tool, co-authoring an ebook, or building a combined SaaS platform. Additionally, interacting with the cybersecurity community on social media, GitHub, or forums can yield insightful input during the development process, guaranteeing that your product satisfies practical requirements. By encouraging teamwork, you may improve the calibre of your products and reach a larger audience of advocates and potential buyers who can help spread the word about them.

3.2 Case Study: The Bug Bounty Millionaire

Bug bounty hunting has the power to change lives and open up incredible employment options, making it much more than just a recreational activity. Santiago Lopez, an ethical hacker from Argentina who made a million dollars from his love of cybersecurity, is a prime illustration of this. Santiago's experience shows that hacking may be both intellectually and monetarily gratifying when done in a morally and legally responsible manner. His experience serves as a testament to the value of perseverance, lifelong learning, and favourable circumstances in the field of cybersecurity.

Despite having little prior expertise, Santiago was determined to become an expert in ethical hacking. He became well-versed in the complexities of cybersecurity and joined sites like HackerOne, which link ethical hackers with businesses looking to find and address security flaws. Santiago's perseverance eventually paid off. He gained a sharp eye for identifying serious defects in important tech systems, and some of the biggest names in the field generously rewarded him for his efforts. His accomplishment serves as a potent reminder that anyone can succeed in bug bounty hunting if they have the correct attitude, abilities, and willpower.

How do you begin, then? The first step for anyone motivated by Santiago's tale and keen to start their own bug bounty adventure is becoming proficient with fundamental cybersecurity technologies. Nmap, Metasploit, and Burp Suite are essential tools for finding and taking advantage of system vulnerabilities. After gaining these abilities, prospective ethical hackers ought to sign up for trustworthy bug bounty programs like Cobalt, HackerOne, Bugcrowd, and Synack. By compensating those who find vulnerabilities, these platforms act as a conduit between hackers and businesses actively working to improve their security.

It's crucial for novices to start small and progressively gain competence. To acquire experience and confidence, beginners should concentrate on lesser-known projects rather than immediately aiming for high-profile enterprises. Examining previous vulnerability reports is another crucial tactic since it offers insights into the methods and mindset of seasoned bug bounty hunters. Furthermore, networking with other industry professionals can provide direction, mentoring, and information on the newest tactics and best practices.

When dealing with top-tier systems, bug bounty hunting might yield significant financial rewards. For legitimate security reports, companies such as Apple, Microsoft, Tesla, Facebook, Google, and others give substantial compensation. In addition to offering financial incentives, these initiatives give participants the chance to work on cutting-edge technologies and help secure popular platforms. However, perseverance and patience are necessary for success in this sector. In order to succeed, bug bounty hunting requires constant learning, flexibility, and a dedication to staying ahead of changing security threats.

A compelling illustration of how bug bounty hunting can transform a person's life is Santiago Lopez's story. Anyone can succeed in this exciting and fulfilling career by learning the necessary skills, joining reliable platforms, starting small, picking up tips from others, and persevering. Significant financial and professional benefits are available to individuals who are prepared to work hard and take on the difficulties of ethical hacking.

Finding High-Paying Clients in Cybersecurity

The secret is to acquire high-paying clients if you want to make money from your cybersecurity expertise outside of bug bounties. The best clients are those that appreciate knowledge and are prepared to pay top price for it, not those who are searching for cheap labour. However, how can one locate them?

Numerous networks match high-paying jobs with cybersecurity experts. Jobs in compliance audits, security consulting, and penetration testing can be found on Upwork. If you specialise in specialised services like vulnerability assessments, Fiverr is a good fit. Platforms like Bugcrowd and HackerOne are great for bug bounty searching for ethical hackers, and Cobalt provides penetration testing possibilities for seasoned pros. Toptal is a premium platform that accepts top-tier specialists if you're looking for high-end security consultancy.

A robust cybersecurity portfolio is essential if you want to stand out and draw in high-paying clients. Start by creating a personal website that features case studies, client endorsements, and your work. You can establish yourself as an authority in the topic by creating blog entries and posting research papers on Medium, LinkedIn, or your personal blog. Participating in open-source projects, particularly those involving tools like Metasploit or OWASP ZAP, increases one's visibility and reputation in the cybersecurity community. Customer reviews are also very helpful; happy customers are your finest advertising, so always gather and showcase them.

It takes more than simply technical expertise to win high-paying clients; strategy is key. Determine your specialisation first. Whether it's bug bounty hunting, compliance advising, or penetration testing, specialisation makes you stand out. To keep your competitive edge, stay current on the newest security trends and certifications. Engage in active participation on cybersecurity blogs, LinkedIn, and Twitter to establish a powerful online profile. Networking is equally crucial; engaging with people in the field, attending cybersecurity conferences, and participating in online groups can lead to profitable prospects. Lastly, take use of referrals. If you produce excellent outcomes, happy customers will gladly recommend you to others, which will help your business expand naturally.

It takes a combination of technical know-how, strategic positioning, and successful networking to find high-paying clients in the cybersecurity industry. Being a thought leader in your field is one of the best strategies to draw in high-end customers. By regularly disseminating insightful information, trends, and solutions via webinars, podcasts, or speeches at trade shows, this can be accomplished. Establishing yourself as the go-to expert helps you gain reputation and become more visible to prospective customers who are prepared to pay for superior knowledge. Working on joint projects or research with other cybersecurity experts can also help you build your name and reach a wider audience.

Knowing your clients' unique wants and adjusting your services to meet them is another essential component of landing high-paying clients. Offering specialised solutions might help you stand out from the competition because many organisations confront different security concerns. For example, some companies could need sophisticated threat detection and response techniques, while others would need compliance with particular rules like GDPR or HIPAA. You can establish yourself as a trusted counsellor rather than merely a service provider by holding in-depth consultations and exhibiting a profound comprehension of their problems. This strategy not only supports greater fees but also cultivates enduring customer relationships based on reliability and output.

Don't undervalue the ability to use technology to expedite your client acquisition procedure. You can effectively handle leads, monitor client interactions, and pursue possible prospects with the use of tools like CRM software. Insights about what appeals to your target audience can also be gained by employing analytics to gauge the success of your marketing initiatives, such as blog traffic, social media participation, or webinar attendance. You can guarantee a consistent flow of lucrative clients that appreciate your experience and are prepared to spend money on superior cybersecurity solutions by consistently improving your tactics and remaining flexible in response to changes in the market.

3.3 Final Thoughts

One of the most profitable industries nowadays is cybersecurity, but success doesn't just happen; you must know how to properly monetise your abilities. The options are unlimited, whether you want to work as a freelancer, consultant, bug bounty hunter, or develop your own cybersecurity solutions. The secret is to act, develop your brand, and keep improving your knowledge.

What is stopping you, then? Take charge of your cybersecurity career by starting today and putting yourself out there!

Chapter 4: Cybersecurity Consulting and Building a Personal Brand

Welcome to the Goldmine of Cybersecurity!

One of the most profitable occupations in the computer sector is cybersecurity consulting. Organisations worldwide are drowning in a sea of security flaws, compliance issues, and cyberthreats. Companies are in dire need of professionals who can assist them navigate the chaos and strengthen their defences in a world where data breaches make headlines virtually every day. Additionally, they are prepared to pay a high price for that knowledge.

There's a catch, though. It takes more than just technical prowess to succeed in cybersecurity consulting. In addition to demonstrating their technical prowess and using complicated jargon, the most successful consultants are able to convert cybersecurity risks into business risks, explain value in a way that decision-makers can grasp, and—above all—develop a personal brand that positions them as the industry authority.

This chapter explores what it truly takes to succeed in cybersecurity consulting, from understanding what clients really need to leveraging compliance frameworks for credibility. It delves into the story of Troy Hunt, a cybersecurity expert who mastered personal branding, and lays out a roadmap for building your own authority in the industry. By the time you finish this chapter, you'll have a clear strategy to establish yourself as a sought-after cybersecurity consultant.

4.1 What Clients Really Want in a Cybersecurity Consultant

Businesses know that cybersecurity is crucial, yet most of them are unsure about what specific measures they need to implement. That's precisely where consultants come in. However, landing a consulting role isn't just about having deep technical expertise. Many highly skilled professionals struggle to get hired because they don't know how to position their skills in a way that resonates with business leaders.

Businesses need someone who can connect cybersecurity with business goals, not just someone with experience in forensic investigation or penetration testing. A consultant must be able to interpret methodological perils into fiscal and operative jeopardies, help organizations comply with legal and regulatory requirements, and offer security recommendations that are both effective and cost-efficient.

For instance, a customer is much more interested in how a well-configured firewall lowers financial risk and guarantees regulatory compliance than a consultant who may be an expert in firewall configuration. Speaking business language is equally as important as speaking security when it comes to cybersecurity advice.

4.2 The Compliance Game: Why It Matters More Than You Think

Compliance is one of the most neglected but important facets of cybersecurity consulting. Strict laws control the operations of sectors including government, healthcare, and banking, and noncompliance can result in severe penalties, legal issues, and harm to one's reputation.

Knowledge of compliance frameworks is a huge plus for cybersecurity consultants. Organisations frequently seek out outside experts who can assist them in adhering to security best practices and certain regulatory needs. Gaining expertise in compliance frameworks increases a consultant's value and offers opportunities to higher-paying jobs.

Some of the most well-known cybersecurity frameworks are as follows.

Framework	Purpose
ISO 27001	International standard for information security management
NIST CSF	U.S. government framework for improving cybersecurity practices
CIS Controls	Security best practices to prevent cyber threats
GDPR	European data privacy regulation
HIPAA	U.S. healthcare security law

Let me give an in-depth understanding of these frameworks along with their importance and use cases.

ISO 27001

A globally accepted standard for information security management systems (ISMS) is ISO 27001. It offers a methodical approach to handling confidential business data, guaranteeing its security through risk management procedures, guidelines, and controls. Due to its broad acceptance across nations and industries, ISO 27001 is a useful certification for businesses doing business abroad. It assists businesses in recognising, evaluating, and reducing information security threats while guaranteeing data availability, confidentiality, and integrity. ISO 27001 accreditation is necessary for several sectors to fulfil contractual or regulatory requirements. A dedication to information security is demonstrated by obtaining ISO 27001 accreditation, which can increase stakeholder and client trust. In order to guarantee that security procedures adapt to new threats, the standard places a strong emphasis on routine audits and upgrades.

NIST CSF (National Institute of Standards and Technology Cybersecurity Framework)

The U.S. government created the optional NIST CSF framework to assist businesses in managing and lowering cybersecurity risks. Identification, Protection, Detection, Reaction, and Recovery are its five main pillars. The framework is a flexible tool for enhancing cybersecurity posture because it can be applied to companies of diverse sizes and industries. It assists businesses in setting cybersecurity priorities according to their unique risks and operational requirements. Alignment with NIST CSF is necessary for compliance with numerous U.S. government agencies and industry. The framework offers recommendations for identifying and handling cyber incidents while reducing downtime and harm. The framework can be used by organisations to evaluate their present level of cybersecurity maturity and pinpoint areas that require development.

CIS Controls (Center for Internet Security Controls)

The CIS Controls are a collection of 18 security best practices that are prioritised and intended to assist organisations in defending against common cyberthreats. A worldwide community of cybersecurity specialists creates them. By ranking the controls according to their efficacy, organisations can prioritise the most important security measures first. They offer doable procedures for putting security measures like malware protection, inventory control, and access control into practice. By addressing the most common attack routes, the measures lower the chance that cyberattacks would be successful. Organisations can more easily fulfil their compliance duties because many of the controls are in line with regulatory standards. Organisations of any size and in any industry can use the controls.

GDPR (General Data Protection Regulation)

The European Union (EU) passed the General Data Protection Regulation (GDPR) to safeguard the personal information of its inhabitants. It is applicable to every organisation, regardless of location, that handles or keeps data about EU citizens. Strict procedures, such as encryption, access controls, and data breach notifications, are required by GDPR to secure personal data. It gives people control over their data, including the ability to view, update, or remove it. GDPR is a global data privacy regulation that even non-EU organisations must follow if they handle the data of EU citizens. Significant fines (up to 4% of worldwide yearly turnover) for noncompliance encourage businesses to give data protection first priority. Adherence to GDPR shows a dedication to privacy, which improves consumer confidence and brand image.

HIPAA (Health Insurance Portability and Accountability Act)

HIPAA is a U.S. legislation that establishes guidelines for safeguarding private patient health information (PHI). It is pertinent to insurers, healthcare providers, and their commercial partners. HIPAA guarantees the secure handling of PHI, and safeguards patient privacy and confidentiality by using technologies such as encryption, access limits, and frequent risk assessments. HIPAA compliance is essential for healthcare organisations to avoid fines and legal action. In the event of a data breach, HIPAA mandates that organisations notify the authorities and impacted individuals. Additionally, the law encourages the safe sharing of medical records, which enhances care coordination and quality.

NIST CSF and ISO 27001, which are both widely accepted in the United States and internationally recognised, offer systematic frameworks for controlling cybersecurity risks. For organisations seeking to put in place actionable security measures, CIS Controls are perfect since they provide a set of prioritised, realistic procedures for protecting against cyber-attacks. Both GDPR and HIPAA are legislative frameworks that handle data privacy and protection; GDPR is applicable globally, whereas HIPAA is only applicable to healthcare data in the United States. When combined, these guidelines and standards assist businesses in creating strong cybersecurity plans, adhering to legal obligations, and safeguarding private information from ever changing dangers. Any company looking to improve its security posture and gain the trust of its partners, consumers, and regulators must have these tools.

There will always be a great need for consultants who can show that they understand these standards and can help companies align their security policies with them. It's critical to emphasise in your cybersecurity service pitch how compliance knowledge may assist businesses stay out of problems with the law while enhancing their security posture.

4.3 How Troy Hunt Became a Cybersecurity Rockstar

Troy Hunt is one of the few cybersecurity experts who has mastered personal branding. Hunt made a reputation for himself in the industry by putting value first. He is the founder of Have I Been Pwned (HIBP), a popular service that lets users verify if their personal data has been compromised.

Developing something helpful, educating the public, and progressively establishing himself as an authority were the steps he took to become a leading cybersecurity consultant rather than promoting his services aggressively. In addition to creating a solution, he also wrote incredibly interesting security blogs that appealed to both business executives and technical experts by simplifying difficult subjects into easily understood insights.

In addition to writing, he gained recognition by giving speeches at some of the largest security conferences, such as Microsoft Ignite, DEF CON, and Black Hat. As he actively participated in the cybersecurity community on sites like LinkedIn and Twitter, his online visibility quickly expanded. His experience and well-known brand eventually brought him collaborations with big companies like Microsoft and a plethora of prestigious consulting possibilities.

The most important lesson to be learnt from Hunt's path is that cybersecurity experts who wish to establish their brand should concentrate on adding value. Instead of merely promoting expertise, the objective is to teach and share ideas through writing, public speaking, and social media involvement. Individuals that continuously make significant contributions to the industry will be acknowledged.

4.4 How to Build Your Personal Brand in Cybersecurity

Better employment offers, increased consultancy fees, and a constant flow of chances can all be accessed with a strong personal brand. Engaging with the community and demonstrating competence on a regular basis are the best ways to establish credibility in cybersecurity.

Among the best methods for doing this are public speaking, blogging, and LinkedIn. Thought leadership can be shown on LinkedIn by sharing case studies, ideas, and security trends. Professionals can provide in-depth technical research and analysis via blogging, whether on own websites or on platforms like Medium. Speaking at webinars and industry events increases visibility and authority even more.

Research publication is another effective tactic. But not all research is successful. Focussing on popular subjects like ransomware, AI security, and zero-trust architecture will help you stand out. Research becomes more impactful and accessible when it is broken down into basic, interesting content and includes real-world case studies. Wider visibility is ensured by sharing discoveries on cybersecurity forums, LinkedIn, and Twitter. Starting a podcast or YouTube channel can be just as successful for people who are not interested in writing. The objective is to get recognition by continuously offering insightful contributions to the field.

4.5 Five Steps to Launching a Cybersecurity Consultancy

There is more to starting a cybersecurity consulting business than just technical know-how. It entails scalable service offerings, efficient outreach, and smart positioning.

Identifying a market niche and developing an attractive value proposition are the initial steps. Being an expert in a certain field, such as compliance, ethical hacking, or cloud security, helps set oneself apart from rivals. The focus is further increased by identifying the appropriate target clientele, such as fintech companies, small businesses, or healthcare providers. A compelling value proposition makes the issue being addressed very evident. An expert in fintech security, for example, would market oneself as someone who "assists fintech companies in securing their AWS cloud and meeting compliance standards."

Establishing an internet presence is essential. Credibility is established by regular content production, a personal website promoting services, and an optimised LinkedIn presence. Testimonials from clients and case studies increase trust.

Offering free security audits to new customers might be a good way to get referrals and develop a portfolio. Contract acquisition is aided by active involvement in cybersecurity networking groups and direct outreach to CISOs and IT managers on LinkedIn.

Creating organised consulting packages increases the scalability of services as the organisation expands. Operations are streamlined by standardised risk assessments, security audits, and training initiatives. In the long run, growing through alliances, security education programs, and automated evaluation systems can boost income and impact.

4.6 Final Thoughts

Cybersecurity consultancy is a business as well as a technological field. Technical proficiency is the cornerstone, but effective communication of security threats to business executives, the development of a strong personal brand, and the application of astute business tactics are what really make a difference. Those who are able to strike this equilibrium will establish themselves as leaders in their field and get lucrative consulting jobs.

Chapter 5: Productizing Your Cybersecurity Knowledge

Cybersecurity is exploding right now. Every company—whether it's a scrappy startup or a Fortune 500 giant—is scrambling to lock down its systems. That means experts who can provide real solutions are in ridiculously high demand. But here's the real question—why just trade your time for money when you could turn your expertise into a scalable digital product? Think about it—ebooks, automation scripts, online courses, even full-blown SaaS solutions. Not only can you establish yourself as a thought leader, but you can also create a steady stream of income that grows beyond the hours you put in.

This chapter is all about turning your cybersecurity knowledge into a product that people will pay for—and doing it in just 30 days. Let's go.

5.1 Turning Expertise into Digital Products

Cybersecurity professionals spend years learning the craft—identifying threats, solving complex security problems, staying one step ahead of hackers. Instead of keeping all that knowledge locked up, why not package it into something valuable that people are willing to buy? There are so many ways to do this.

Some choose to write cybersecurity eBooks, reports, and mini-courses. If you've got deep expertise in ethical hacking, compliance, or threat intelligence, why not turn that knowledge into an ebook? Platforms like Amazon KDP, Gumroad, and Leanpub make it easy to self-publish and start selling. If you're better at explaining things through video, consider launching short, niche-focused courses on Udemy, Teachable, or Coursera. Or, if you've done in-depth research on vulnerabilities or compliance frameworks, you could sell exclusive reports on a subscription basis or through direct sales.

Take the example of a security researcher who discovered vulnerabilities in IoT devices. Instead of just writing a blog post, they compiled their findings into a 100-page *IoT Security Handbook* and sold it for $49 per copy on Gumroad and LinkedIn. Three months later, they had made over $10,000—without ever needing to book a single consulting gig.

Beyond writing, another profitable path is developing security automation tools and SaaS solutions. If you've built scripts to automate vulnerability assessments, why not package them into a tool or SaaS platform? Threat intelligence dashboards are another goldmine—CISOs and security teams would pay good money for real-time insights. And let's not forget compliance checkers—businesses struggle with GDPR, ISO 27001, and SOC 2 requirements. A tool that simplifies the process could be a game-changer.

A great example? A cybersecurity consultant built a simple WordPress security scanner and launched it as a freemium tool. Within six months, over 20,000 users had signed up, and premium features brought in an annual revenue of $100,000. Not bad for a side project!

5.2 Case Study: Burp Suite's Rise to Industry Leadership

One of the biggest success stories in cybersecurity productization is Burp Suite. What started as a simple penetration testing tool is now *the* gold standard for web security testing.

So, how did Burp Suite become a giant? First, it solved a real pain point—early pen testers struggled with manual security testing, so Burp Suite automated the process, making life significantly easier. It also followed the freemium-to-enterprise model, offering a free version to attract users while keeping advanced features behind a paywall. The cybersecurity community played a huge role in its growth, as security pros recommended it through forums, hacking communities, and conferences. Finally, PortSwigger, the company behind Burp Suite, kept innovating—regular updates, AI-driven security scanning, and automation ensured it stayed ahead of competitors. The key lessons here? Solve a real problem. Offer a freemium model to hook users. Keep improving based on customer feedback. And most importantly, tap into the cybersecurity community for growth.

5.3 Monetization Models: How to Make Money

Now that you have a product idea, how do you actually get paid? There are several ways to monetize cybersecurity products, each with its own pros and cons.

Model	Pros	Cons	Best For
One-Time Payment	Quick cash, no long-term maintenance	No recurring revenue, always need new customers	eBooks, one-time tools, pen testing scripts
Subscription (SaaS Model)	Recurring revenue = financial stability	Needs continuous updates and support	SaaS tools, compliance platforms, security scanning services
Freemium (Basic Free, Paid Upgrades)	Attracts a big user base fast	High infrastructure costs, not all users upgrade	Web security scanners, API security tools, open-source

Let me give you a detailed breakdown of the monetization models for cybersecurity products.

One-Time Payment Model

To use the product or service, customers must pay a single, upfront charge. This simple concept is frequently applied to digital items such as tools, scripts, and eBooks. The benefits are numerous. ♣ Quick cash flow from sales, which is perfect for financing marketing or additional development. ♣ Without the need for ongoing customer assistance or recurring billing systems, it is simple to set up and maintain. ♣ There is no requirement to offer ongoing support or upgrades once the product is sold, unless specifically stated. This paradigm does have certain drawbacks, though. ♣ Revenue is restricted to one-time sales, necessitating ongoing efforts to draw in new clients. ♣ The product's market may eventually become saturated, making steady sales more difficult to achieve. ♣ If you don't release fresh products or upgrades, customers might not come back. This model is best for educational content like ethical hacking guides or compliance manuals; penetration testing scripts, vulnerability scanners, or standalone software; and specialized tools or resources that cater to a specific audience. For example, a cybersecurity researcher sells a Zero-Day Exploitation Course for $299 per user, generating $250,000 in six months. This model works well for high-value, knowledge-based products.

Subscription (SaaS Model)

Customers pay a recurring fee (monthly or annually) to access the product or service. This model is commonly used for Software as a Service (SaaS) platform. The benefits include: ♣ recurring revenue providing a predictable and stable income stream, which is great for long-term financial planning; ♣ customer retention that encourages long-term relationships with customers, as they continue paying for ongoing access; ♣ easier to scale as the customer base grows, with the potential for upselling or cross-selling additional features. This model is not devoid of disadvantages. It requires regular updates, bug fixes, and customer support to retain subscribers. Developing and maintaining a SaaS platform can be resource-intensive. Customers may cancel subscriptions if they don't see ongoing value, leading to revenue loss. This model is best for SaaS tools like Vulnerability scanners, compliance platforms, or log monitoring tools; managed services like Security monitoring, threat intelligence, or incident response platforms; and Subscription-based access to cybersecurity training or certification courses. For example, A cybersecurity firm builds a phishing simulation platform with a $39/month subscription model. Within a year, they attract over 2,000 paying subscribers, generating significant recurring revenue.

Freemium (Basic Free, Paid Upgrades)

The basic version of the product is offered for free, while advanced features or premium tiers require payment. This model is popular for tools and platforms with a wide user base. This model has several; pros: ♣ attracts a large audience quickly by offering free access, increasing brand visibility and market penetration; ♣ free users can be converted into paying customers by demonstrating the value of premium features; ♣ free users can provide feedback, contribute to open-source projects, or help improve the product. The limitations are: ♣ supporting a large number of free users can be expensive, especially for cloud-based services; ♣ not all free users will upgrade to paid plans, which can make it challenging to monetize effectively; ♣ requires careful design of free and paid tiers to ensure the free version is useful but not too limiting. This model is best suited for free basic web scans with paid options for in-depth analysis or advanced features; free tier for small-scale usage, with paid plans for enterprise-level needs of API security; free community edition with a premium version offering additional functionality or support in open-source projects. For example, a cybersecurity startup offers a free web vulnerability scanner with limited features. Users who need advanced scanning capabilities or enterprise-level support can upgrade to a paid plan, generating revenue from premium users.

Comparison and Strategic Use

One-Time Payment is deal for quick cash flow and low-maintenance products but lacks long-term revenue potential. Best for niche or knowledge-based products. Subscription (SaaS) provides stable, recurring revenue but requires ongoing investment in product maintenance and customer support. Best for tools and platforms that offer continuous value. Freemium is great for building a large user base and creating upsell opportunities but can be costly to maintain. Best for tools with broad appeal and scalable infrastructure.

Real-World Examples

♣ **One-Time Payment:** A cybersecurity specialist makes a substantial upfront profit by charging $500 per licence for a penetration testing toolkit.

♣ **Subscription:** A business generates a consistent revenue stream from enterprise clients by charging $99/month for a cloud security monitoring platform. ♣ **Freemium:** A community edition of an open-source vulnerability scanner is available for free, but a commercial version with more capabilities and support costs $49 per month.

You may increase revenue and build a long-lasting cybersecurity company by selecting the best monetisation model for your product, target market, and corporate objectives. These models have generated significant profits for numerous cybersecurity businesses. In one instance, a researcher made $250,000 in six months by selling a Zero-Day Exploitation Course for $299 per customer. A phishing simulation tool with a $39/month subscription model was developed by another cybersecurity company. They had more than 2,000 paying subscribers in less than a year.

5.4 Actionable Plan: Launching a Cybersecurity Product in 30 Days

How does one move from concept to launch in a month? This is a road map:

Start with market research and idea validation in *Week 1*. Determine what makes your product special, investigate rivals, and identify a cybersecurity issue that customers need resolved. Before you construct anything, test demand using surveys or polls on LinkedIn. W*eek 2* is dedicated to product development. Select a format, such as an automated script, SaaS tool, eBook, or mini-course. Construct a Minimum Viable Product (MVP) and get preliminary input. Create a landing page and gather pre-launch registrations. By *Week 3*, turn your attention to marketing and branding. Create an account on Medium, Twitter, and LinkedIn. Post informative blog entries to draw readers in, and provide free trials or early discounts to get traction. Finally, launch time comes in *Week 4*. Promote your product on websites such as your own or on sites like Gumroad, Udemy, and AWS Marketplace. To increase sales, use LinkedIn outreach and email marketing. Get reviews and use the comments to improve your product.

5.5 Final Thought: Stop Trading Time for Money

There is more to the cybersecurity sector than working 9 to 5 and looking for consultancy jobs. You may create several revenue streams, assist companies in maintaining their security, and position yourself as an industry leader by turning your knowledge into a digital product. All of this is possible while earning a substantial salary.

What're you waiting for, then? Create your cybersecurity empire by getting started now.

Part II   Cybersecurity Opportunities

Chapter 6: Corporate Cybersecurity Roles and How to Get Hired

There are many cybersecurity careers existing, but how can you land one? It's a completely different battle. Businesses are in dire need of qualified workers, but they continue to turn away excellent applicants due to antiquated hiring practices, malfunctioning HR filters, and degree bias. On the other side, talented individuals—many of them self-taught—get caught in an endless loop of applications, rejections, and ghosted interviews. The hiring process is fundamentally broken, and while that sounds frustrating, it also presents an opportunity. If you understand how the system works and learn how to bypass the traditional gatekeepers, you can position yourself as a top pick for high-paying cybersecurity roles—whether you're starting from scratch, switching careers, or aiming for an advanced security position. This chapter is all about cutting through the noise and showing you real, actionable strategies to land your dream cybersecurity job.

6.1 Why Companies Struggle to Find Cybersecurity Talent

Given the increasing wave of cyber threats, you'd assume that companies would be hiring cybersecurity professionals at an unprecedented rate. And they are—but they're going about it all wrong. The problem isn't a lack of talent; it's a flawed hiring process that filters out the very professionals, companies desperately need. Instead of identifying the best candidates, most hiring systems are built to eliminate as many applicants as possible.

One of the biggest barriers is the overuse of automated resume screeners—Applicant Tracking Systems (ATS). These systems scan resumes for specific keywords, often rejecting highly skilled candidates simply because their wording doesn't match the software's rigid criteria. Then there's the outdated degree bias. Many companies still require a computer science or cybersecurity degree, even though real-world security work has little to do with traditional academic coursework. Some of the best cybersecurity professionals are self-taught, yet they're routinely overlooked because they don't have a formal degree.

And let's talk about job descriptions—many of them are completely unrealistic. Companies frequently post requirements that ask for expertise in ethical hacking, cloud security, AI, blockchain, quantum computing, and more—essentially demanding five different career paths in one person. It's no wonder they struggle to fill positions. In fact, a CyberSeek study found that over 600,000 cybersecurity jobs remain unfilled simply because companies refuse to consider non-traditional but highly capable candidates.

It's like companies are trying to find a unicorn in a field full of racehorses. They're so hung up on checking boxes—degrees, certifications, buzzwords—that they're missing out on the very people who could save their bacon when the next big breach hits. The irony? Some of the most talented cybersecurity pros out there are the ones who've been hacking systems (ethically, of course) since they were teenagers, not the ones who spent four years memorizing textbooks. But because they don't fit the "perfect candidate" mold, they get tossed aside by algorithms that couldn't spot real talent if it slapped them in the face. It's like using a sledgehammer to crack a nut—sure, it'll get the job done, but you're destroying everything valuable in the process.

And don't even get me started on those job descriptions. They're like a wish list from someone who's watched too many hacker movies. "Must have 10 years of experience in a technology that's only existed for five." "Must be an expert in every single niche of cybersecurity, plus know how to code, plus have a PhD in quantum physics." It's laughable. No wonder there are hundreds of thousands of unfilled jobs. Companies are so busy looking for a mythical "perfect" candidate that they're ignoring the real, capable, and hungry professionals right in front of them. The truth is, the cybersecurity world doesn't need more gatekeepers—it needs more problem-solvers. And if companies don't wake up and fix their broken hiring systems, they're going to keep getting hacked while the talent they need sits on the sidelines, waiting for a chance to shine.

6.2 How a Self-Taught Security Analyst Landed a $300K Job

If there's one person who proves you don't need to follow the traditional path to land a high-paying cybersecurity job, it's Alex Carter. He had no degree, no corporate IT background, and no formal training—yet today, he works as a senior security engineer at a Fortune 500 company, making over $300,000 a year.

Alex started his journey with bug bounties, finding security vulnerabilities in major companies like Tesla and Microsoft. Instead of waiting for someone to give him an opportunity, he created his own by documenting his findings and writing about security exploits on his blog. His posts gained traction, and soon, hiring managers began noticing him. He didn't waste time applying mindlessly through malfunctioning HR systems, in contrast to most job seekers. Rather than using a boilerplate CV, he used LinkedIn to reach out to hiring managers directly and demonstrate his abilities using instances from the real world.

Alex wasted time acquiring generic IT qualifications that had little bearing on his career. He immediately pursued the prestigious OSCP (Offensive Security Certified Professional) credential, which attested to his practical penetration testing skills. He referred to his Capture The Flag (CTF) challenges and bug bounty reports, which were considerably more credible than any conventional resume, when employers sought evidence of his abilities.

Alex's narrative demonstrates that employers are looking for problem solvers, not just degree holders. Skills are more important in cybersecurity than certificates. Even if you lack a formal background, you can still acquire a high-paying job provided you can demonstrate your competence.

6.3 Beating the Hiring System

How can one duplicate Alex's success, then? How do you convince employers to notice your skills and get around the flawed hiring system? The first thing to understand is that certifications and experience matter in different ways. If you're looking for a corporate security job—especially in compliance, governance, or risk management—certifications like CISSP or CISM can help you stand out. But if you're going into hacking, penetration testing, or offensive security, real-world skills are far more valuable than a stack of generic IT certifications. Certifications like OSCP, CEH, AWS Security, and GCIH offer high ROI and can make a real difference in your job prospects.

However, certifications alone won't land you the job. Networking is crucial. LinkedIn and Twitter (X) are powerful tools for cybersecurity professionals—engaging with industry leaders, commenting on posts, and sharing insights can make you visible to recruiters and hiring managers. Attending cybersecurity events like DEF CON and Black Hat is another major advantage. These conferences are goldmines for networking, and a single conversation with the right person can lead to a job offer. Another way to stand out is by contributing to open-source security projects. Many companies look at GitHub or other repositories to see what cybersecurity professionals are working on. By contributing to open-source projects, you're building credibility while showcasing your skills.

Referrals for jobs are even more successful than networking. The majority of businesses give internal recommendations precedence over job board applications. Rather than applying mindlessly, concentrate on establishing connections with industry experts. You have a much higher chance of passing HR screening and getting an interview if you are referred by someone in the organisation.

6.4 The Fast-Track Plan to Landing a Cybersecurity Job

You may differentiate yourself from other job seekers by following a five-step strategy if you want to get into cybersecurity rapidly. Start by building a portfolio or blog about security that highlights your work. Whether it's vulnerability reports, hacking courses, or security research, having an internet presence helps hiring managers and recruiters find you. Second, sign up for bug bounty sites such as Bugcrowd and HackerOne. Through these platforms, you can demonstrate your abilities in practical situations, and employers regularly hire top performers.

Third, include cybersecurity keywords to your LinkedIn profile to help recruiters locate you. Hiring managers frequently look for specialised talents like "cloud security," "penetration testing," or "incident response." You'll be more likely to be contacted about employment openings if these terms are included in your profile. Fourth, look for employers who value skill-based hiring over antiquated resume screening. Instead of depending solely on qualifications, some employers assess candidates' practical skills using CTF-style hiring challenges. Lastly, don't be scared to send hiring supervisors a direct cold message. Traditional applications won't open doors, but a brief, well-written pitch that highlights your strengths as a team player can.

Let's face it, cybersecurity is an attitude as much as a profession. It all comes down to being the one who spots systemic flaws before they become obvious holes. And you know what? Businesses are in dire need of somebody like that. The worst part is that they don't always seek for the candidate with the longest résumé or the most expensive degree. They are searching for someone who can demonstrate that they have the skills necessary to defend their systems against the always changing threats that exist in the world. Here's where you can help. By adhering to the fast-track approach, you are presenting yourself as the answer to their issues rather than merely seeking for jobs. You become more than just another applicant when you accomplish that; you become the one they can't afford to overlook.

Let's now discuss the key ingredient: confidence. Yes, I did hear you. Although it helps, being confident is more than merely entering a room as though you own it. It all comes down to being aware of and capable of demonstrating your value. Not only do you demonstrate your abilities when you blog about security trends, crush bug bounties, or send a compelling direct message to a hiring manager, but you also demonstrate your courage to take the initiative. And that kind of confidence is invaluable in a field where quick thinking is half the game. Therefore, don't wait for approval. Start networking, start developing your brand, and start showcasing your abilities to the world.

6.5 Final Thoughts

The hiring process for cybersecurity is flawed, but that's precisely why you can exploit it. You'll be caught in a never-ending cycle of rejections and cancelled interviews if you only use standard job applications. However, even without a formal background, you can acquire a high-paying cybersecurity job if you adopt a calculated strategy, demonstrating your abilities, networking in the appropriate areas, and avoiding out-of-date recruiting filters. Skilled experts are needed in the market, and those who can effectively demonstrate their knowledge will always have an advantage. Lastly, keep in mind that the rules of the game are being changed daily and that the cybersecurity industry is evolving more quickly than ever before. The gatekeepers of the old school, those who are only interested in credentials and degrees, are slipping. What is replacing them? a new employment culture that prioritises abilities, ingenuity, and drive. That's your lucky charm. You're not merely playing the game; you're altering it by concentrating on your abilities rather than what's written down. Go out there, create a stir, and demonstrate to them why you are the cybersecurity industry's future. Not only is the job you desire waiting for you, but it is also yours to have.

Chapter 7: Freelancing vis-a-vis Full-Time Cybersecurity Jobs

So, you're diving into the world of cybersecurity, but now you're at a crossroads. Do you stick with the security (no pun intended) of a full-time job, or do you take the leap and become your own boss as a freelancer? Both paths come with their own perks—and their own headaches. The real question is: what kind of life do you want to live?

In this chapter, we'll break it all down. We'll look at the pros and cons of each route, what you can expect in terms of work, money, and career growth, and the story of a freelancer who turned his cybersecurity skills into a $500K-per-year business. And if you're leaning toward freelancing, we'll give you a step-by-step guide to building a six-figure cybersecurity hustle without the constant stress of wondering where your next paycheck is coming from.

7.1 The 9-to-5 Cybersecurity Career: Stability and Growth

A full-time cybersecurity job is great if you thrive on structure. You get a steady paycheck, benefits, and a clear career path. Plus, you'll have access to company-funded training and high-end security tools that you probably wouldn't buy on your own.

Many cybersecurity professionals find themselves in roles like security analysts, penetration testers, SOC analysts, and, for the lucky few, CISOs (Chief Information Security Officers). The advantages? Predictable income, solid networking opportunities, and employer-paid certifications that can boost your career. But let's be real—the corporate grind isn't for everyone. You have fixed work hours, limited control over your projects, and, of course, office politics. Promotions can be slow, and salary jumps often come at the mercy of annual performance reviews.

A full-time gig can feel like golden handcuffs. Sure, the stability is nice, but it comes with strings attached. You're trading freedom for predictability, and for some, that trade-off works. But for others, it's a slow burn. You might find yourself stuck in endless meetings, waiting for approvals, or dealing with red tape that makes even the simplest tasks feel like climbing Mount Everest. And let's not forget the dreaded "corporate ladder." Climbing it can feel like running on a treadmill—you're putting in the work, but you're not always moving forward. If you're someone who craves autonomy and wants to call the shots, the 9-to-5 life might leave you feeling restless, no matter how cushy the benefits are.

That's why so many cybersecurity pros are breaking free and going freelance. Imagine setting your own hours, choosing the projects that excite you, and getting paid what you're actually worth—without waiting for a boss to sign off on it. Freelancing lets you turn your skills into a business, not just a job. Sure, it's not all sunshine and rainbows. You'll have to hustle for clients, manage your own taxes, and deal with the occasional dry spell. The nastiest part is that when you're in charge, the possibilities are endless. You're creating a legacy in addition to a career. And that is more valuable than any corner office or yearly evaluation for people who thrive on independence and adaptability.

7.2 Freelancing in Cybersecurity: Be Your Own Boss

Now, freelancing could be your passport to success if you enjoy the concept of picking your own clients, determining your own hours, and having no revenue cap. Freelancers in cybersecurity work with companies all over the world on projects including compliance advice, security audits, and penetration testing. The finest aspect? You can charge what you're worth and work from any location.

Freelancers are not confined to waiting for a rise from their employer. Rather, as their level of experience increases, so do their fees. Some focus on in-demand fields including incident response, SOC consultancy, and cloud security evaluations. However, there is a cost. Freelancing entails working hard to attract clients, as opposed to a regular job where money comes into your account every two weeks. There's no company-sponsored training, and you have to handle contracts, invoices, and marketing yourself.

Freelancing isn't just a job—it's a lifestyle. You're not just a cybersecurity pro; you're a business owner. That means you get to call the shots. Want to take a Wednesday off to hit the beach? Go for it. Prefer working late nights because that's when you're most productive? No one's stopping you. The freedom is intoxicating, but it comes with a side of responsibility. You've got to stay on top of your game, constantly learning new skills and staying ahead of the latest threats. And yeah, you'll have to deal with the not-so-glamorous stuff—like chasing down late payments or figuring out how to market yourself without sounding like a used car salesman. But for those who thrive on independence, it's a small price to pay for living life on your own terms.

And let's talk about the money. Freelancing isn't just about earning a pay check—it's about unlocking your earning potential. When you're freelancing, your income isn't capped by some corporate pay scale. If you're good at what you do, you can charge premium rates, especially in high-demand niches like cloud security or incident response. The more you hustle, the more you earn. Plus, you can scale your business by taking on bigger clients, hiring a team, or even creating your own cybersecurity tools or courses. Sure, it's not all smooth sailing—there will be lean months and tough clients—but for those with the grit and vision to make it work, freelancing can be the ultimate career hack. It's not just a job; it's your empire in the making.

Aspect	Full-Time Job	Freelancing
Income Stability	Fixed salary, benefits, bonuses	Income fluctuates based on clients and projects
Flexibility	Set work hours, often rigid schedules	Choose when and where to work
Earning Potential	Limited growth without promotions	Unlimited potential, scalable income
Job Security	Stable but dependent on employer	No long-term security, self-reliant
Learning Curve	Structured training, company resources	Must stay updated independently
Independence	Work under management	Freedom to choose projects and clients
Networking	Internal company networking	Global exposure to clients
Work Pressure	Deadlines, office politics, meetings	Client deadlines but fewer workplace politics

7.3 How David Turned Freelancing into a $500K Business

Meet David. A few years ago, he was a cybersecurity analyst in a corporate job, but he always felt like he was worth more. So, he took the leap into freelancing on Upwork. It wasn't easy at first—he struggled to land clients. But once he figured out how to stand out, his earnings skyrocketed. Within three years, he was consistently making $40,000 per month in cybersecurity consulting fees.

Here's how he did it:

First, he picked a niche. He focused on penetration testing, compliance audits (SOC 2, ISO 27001), and cloud security. Then, he optimized his Upwork profile with a strong headline and highlighted his experience. Initially, he charged $150 an hour but later moved to fixed-price projects ranging from $2,500 to $10,000.

Getting those first clients was tough. He started with small $500 jobs just to build reviews. He also provided free security reports to show his value. Once he had a few satisfied clients, referrals started rolling in.

As his reputation grew, he scaled his business. He focused on long-term contracts, gradually raised his rates, and even hired junior analysts to handle smaller tasks. Eventually, he expanded beyond Upwork—launching a cybersecurity blog, a YouTube channel, and even an online course for passive income.

The result? Within three years, he hit $500K per year in cybersecurity consulting fees. Not bad for a guy who started with a few $500 gigs.

7.4 How to Start Your Own 6-Figure Cybersecurity Freelance Business
Want to follow in David's footsteps? Here's the game plan:

Step 1: Pick a High-Demand Niche - Let's be real—you can't be everything to everyone. The cybersecurity world is massive, and trying to tackle all of it at once is a surefire way to burn out before you even get started. Instead, zero in on a niche that's hot right now. Think of it like this: businesses are drowning in cyber threats, and they're looking for lifeguards who specialize in specific areas. Web application security testing? That's like being the guy who can spot the cracks in a company's digital front door. Cloud security audits? You're the one making sure their data isn't floating around in the ether, ripe for the picking. SOC 2 compliance? You're the rulebook guru who keeps them out of legal trouble. Digital forensics? You're the cyber detective solving crimes after the fact. Pick something you're passionate about, but more importantly, pick something businesses are willing to pay big bucks for.

Step 2: Build an Online Presence - Here's the deal: if you're not online, you don't exist. Period. Your LinkedIn profile isn't just a digital resume—it's your billboard to the world. Optimize it with keywords like "freelance cybersecurity expert" or "cloud security consultant" so recruiters and clients can find you. But don't stop there. Build a simple website that screams, "I'm the person you need to protect your business." It doesn't have to be fancy—just clear, professional, and packed with the services you offer. Then, get yourself on platforms like Upwork, Fiverr, and Toptal. These are your hunting grounds for clients. Think of them as the malls where businesses go shopping for cybersecurity talent. Be there, be visible, and make it impossible for them to scroll past you.

Step 3: Start Small and Build a Reputation - Here's the hard truth: no one's going to hand you a 10,000 contract on day one. You've got to earn your stripes. Start small—take on those $500 to $1,000 gigs that might not make you rich but will make you credible. Treat every job like it's your Super Bowl. Overdeliver, blow their expectations out of the water, and leave them thinking, "Wow, I need to hire this person again." Reviews are your currency in the freelance world. The more five-star ratings you rack up, the more clients will trust you. And trust? That's what turns one-time gigs into long-term relationships.

Step 4: Increase Rates and Secure Recurring Clients - Once you've got a few wins under your belt, it's time to level up. Raise your rates—because you're worth it. But don't just stop at one-off projects. Offer subscription-based services like monthly security audits or vulnerability scans. Businesses love predictability, and if you can lock them into a recurring payment model, you've got yourself a steady income stream. Upsell them on additional services like employee security training or incident response planning. It will be more difficult for them to envision their company operating without you the more value you offer..

Step 5: Scale and Automate - It's time to level up after you've achieved a few victories. Increase your prices since you are valuable. Don't limit yourself to one-off initiatives, though. Provide subscription-based services, such as vulnerability scans or monthly security assessments. Businesses enjoy consistency, so if you can get them to commit to a recurring payment plan, you'll have a reliable source of cash. Offer them extra services like incident response planning or staff security training. It will be more difficult for them to envision their company operating without you the more value you offer. What're you waiting for, then? The freelance cybersecurity market is open, and the winners are the ones who work hard. Your six-figure business is a plan waiting to be realised, not just a pipe dream. Go ahead and make it happen.

7.5 Final Thoughts

Both full-time cybersecurity jobs and freelancing have their ups and downs. If you value stability, benefits, and structured career growth, go for the corporate route. However, freelancing might be the best choice you ever make if you're looking for independence, the possibility of earning more money, and control over your work. Whatever route you go on, cybersecurity is a fascinating industry with high demand, so act now and begin creating your ideal job!

Chapter 8: Cybersecurity Startups and Entrepreneurship

For good reason, cybersecurity is one of the most popular industries at the moment; companies are rushing to find cutting-edge security solutions as cyber threats increase. However, a startling 90% of cybersecurity firms fail within the first few years, despite the skyrocketing demand. Why? They either struggle to differentiate themselves from the competition, fail to verify their market, or are unable to scale quickly enough.

This chapter will outline the most frequent causes of cybersecurity company failure, examine how CrowdStrike grew to become a $10 billion industry titan, and provide a step-by-step approach on how to validate a cybersecurity business idea in as little as four weeks. This is your guide to avoiding common mistakes and positioning yourself for success if you're considering starting your own cybersecurity firm.

8.1 Why Do 90% of Cybersecurity Startups Fail?

Although starting a cybersecurity business may seem like a dream, the reality is harsh. Giants like Palo Alto Networks, Cisco, and FireEye dominate the market, which is extremely competitive. Newcomers frequently misjudge the difficulties and make crucial errors that ultimately result in failure. Let's examine the main causes of cybersecurity startups failing.

First of all, a lot of entrepreneurs develop things without first making sure there is a real market for them. Rather than addressing actual cybersecurity issues, they construct based on what they believe to be a good idea. Imagine creating an intrusion detection system with AI capabilities only to discover that businesses already have efficient solutions and don't require another one. In order to prevent this, it is essential to speak with security teams, IT managers, and Chief Information Security Officers (CISOs) to find out what issues are truly keeping them up at night. Another major problem is overcomplicating technology. Cybersecurity startups love to develop cutting-edge tools, but many fail to make them user-friendly. A security platform with top-tier threat detection is useless if companies struggle to implement it. The key? Simplicity. Security teams want tools that integrate smoothly into their existing workflows—not ones that require a PhD to operate. Then there's the issue of failing to stand out. Cybersecurity is crowded. If your product is just another firewall, SIEM tool, or antivirus software, why would customers switch from what they're already using? Startups that thrive are the ones that offer something genuinely different—whether it's faster threat detection, lower costs, or a niche specialization tailored to a specific industry.

And let's not forget about sales and marketing. Many cybersecurity founders are tech geniuses but overlook the importance of selling their product. Spending years perfecting a security solution means nothing if you don't have a clear strategy to attract customers. The best approach? Start selling before your product is even finished. Build relationships, run webinars, and create content that positions you as an authority in the space. Finally, money—or the lack of it—can sink a startup. Many companies raise millions in venture capital, burn through it too fast on development and hiring, and run out of cash before they ever make a profit. The best way to avoid this? Keep costs lean, prioritize early revenue, and don't scale too quickly until you've validated your business model.

8.2 Case Study: How CrowdStrike Became a $10 Billion Company

Let's talk about one of cybersecurity's biggest success stories— CrowdStrike. This company, which George Kurtz founded in 2011, revolutionised endpoint security and grew to be a billion-dollar behemoth. But how were they able to achieve it?

Kurtz identified a huge market niche. Conventional antivirus programs used system resources and were reactive and slow. By creating a lightweight, cloud-based security platform that employed behavioural analysis and artificial intelligence (AI) in place of antiquated signature-based detection, CrowdStrike revolutionised the market. The lesson? Determine the shortcomings of current solutions and create a solution that addresses a critical issue. CrowdStrike made a full commitment to the cloud, in contrast to previous security products that needed intricate on-premise installations. They benefited greatly from this in terms of scalability, deployment simplicity, and a seamless user experience. When developing a cybersecurity firm, think about utilising cloud-native and AI-driven technology to stay ahead of the curve.

Another brilliant move? Their business plan. CrowdStrike used a subscription-based SaaS (Software-as-a-Service) strategy with adjustable pricing in place of conventional software licensing. Businesses found it simpler to sign up without having to pay large upfront fees as a result. Consider how a recurring income model might increase the sustainability of your company if you're starting from scratch. CrowdStrike's success was also greatly influenced by marketing. By conducting webinars, issuing in-depth danger reports, and teaching companies about new cyberthreats, they established themselves as thought leaders. Establishing credibility in the field is a great method to draw clients and win their trust.

Finally, they were able to scale quickly thanks to clever alliances. CrowdStrike made it simple for companies to use their products by integrating with cloud providers like Microsoft and AWS. Positioning with recognized platforms can open doors to enterprise clienteles and drive development at an enhanced pace.

8.3 How to Validate a Cybersecurity Business Idea in 4 Weeks

Have a startup idea in cybersecurity? Make sure there is actual demand before investing time and resources in development. Here's a four-week crash course on how to do it right.

Week 1: Research & Idea Validation. Here's the deal: you can't just throw spaghetti at the wall and hope it sticks. You've got to know exactly what problem you're solving—and for whom. Start by diving deep into the cybersecurity world. Talk to security pros, CISOs, and even IT managers. Ask them what keeps them up at night. Is it ransomware? Compliance headaches? Cloud security nightmares? Take notes, because these pain points are your golden ticket. Then, scope out the competition. What are they offering, and more importantly, what are they missing? Maybe they're all focused on enterprise-level solutions, leaving small businesses in the dust. Or maybe their tools are so complicated, they're practically unusable. Find that gap, and make it your mission to fill it. Your unique value proposition isn't just a fancy buzzword—it's your secret weapon. Nail this, and you're already ahead of the game.

Don't fall in love with your idea just yet. Validate it. Run it by the people who actually deal with these problems every day. If they light up and say, "Yes, I need this!"— you have a good idea. Should they shrug and respond, "Meh," it's time to start over. Recall that this is about what your clients need, not what you think is great. You're setting the groundwork for something significant if you do this step correctly.

Week 2: Prototype & Early Feedback. It's time to get your hands dirty now. The secret is that you may begin receiving feedback without having a finished product. You really don't require a product at all. It may be sufficient to test the waters with a straightforward landing page, a mockup, or simply a one-pager outlining your idea. Here, validation is more important than perfection. See whether your concept is a hit by putting it out there. Engage in outreach to prospective clients via email, LinkedIn, or traditional networking methods. Directly ask them, "Would you pay for this?" Don't mince words; if the response is no, find out why. Is it the cost? The characteristics? how it's displayed? This feedback is absolutely invaluable.

Don't get self-protective. If people aren't taking, it's not a fiasco—it's a learning opportunity. Maybe your idea needs a tweak, or maybe it's time to pivot entirely. The key is to stay flexible and keep iterating. Remember, some of the most successful products started as something completely different. Stay open, stay curious, and keep refining until you hit that sweet spot where your solution meets a real, urgent need.

Week 3: Market Testing. Now it's time to turn up the heat. Run a small-scale marketing campaign to see if there's actual demand for your idea. This could be anything from LinkedIn ads to a blog post series or even a webinar. The goal? To see if people are willing to engage. Do they sign up for your waiting list? Do they click through to learn more? Do they actually show up to your webinar? These are all indications that you're on the right track. But here's the thing: don't just sit back and wait for the magic to happen. Track everything. Which ads perform best? What content gets the most engagement? Use this statistics to fine-tune your tactic.

Additionally, don't be scared to try new things. Your LinkedIn ads may be a huge success even if your first webinar fails. Or perhaps you get a tonne of interest once your blog piece goes viral. The secret is to remain flexible and adjust in response to new information. This is about testing, learning, and optimising, not about spending money on advertisements and crossing your fingers. You should know by the end of this week whether there is a genuine need for your solution and, if so, how to effectively reach your target market.

Week 4: First Sales & Next Steps. Congratulations if you've reached this point; you're prepared to jump in. Give early adopters access to a beta version of your solution. These individuals have been following your journey, interacting with your material, and expressing interest in you. Give them a preview of your creation and observe their reaction. Try out several pricing structures, such as a subscription, one-time charge, or even a freemium model. Seeing what sticks is the aim here. Will people pay? What is the amount? What aspects of your offering do they like (or dislike)?

The true query, though, is: what comes next? You will have to choose between going all in or pivoting based on the sales statistics and feedback. It's time to scale up if the feedback is overwhelmingly positive. Begin developing your product, honing your advertising plan, and getting ready for release. Don't panic if the reaction is ambivalent; it may simply indicate that you need to modify your strategy. Perhaps it's a new feature, a different target market, or a different approach to pricing. The secret is to continue iterating and remaining agile. Keep in mind that this is only the beginning and not the end. You are constructing a business, not only a product. And you're unstoppable if you have the correct attitude.

8.4 Final Thoughts

Although it's difficult, starting a cybersecurity firm is not impossible. Avoiding frequent blunders, taking advice from businesses like CrowdStrike, and following a methodical validation procedure before making a big commitment are all crucial to success. You can create a cybersecurity company that not only endures but flourishes in this cutthroat sector if you have the correct plan, a thorough awareness of consumer demands, and the flexibility to change with the times.

Chapter 9: The Future of Cybersecurity—AI, Blockchain, and Web3

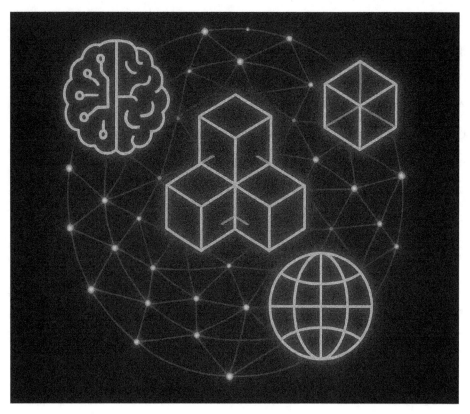

Cyber dangers are changing at a faster rate than ever before, causing a seismic shift in the digital landscape. Once thought to be adequate, traditional security techniques are increasingly unable to keep up with the growing complexity of assaults. As a result, a new era of cybersecurity is beginning, one that is driven by Web3 technologies, blockchain, and artificial intelligence (AI). These developments are not only changing the way threats are identified and countered, but they are also changing the fundamentals of cybersecurity. The foundations of the future are turning out to be Web3's trustless architectures, blockchain's decentralised security features, and AI-driven threat detection. Cybersecurity experts need to keep up with the latest tactics and knowledge to protect digital assets and infrastructures, just as hackers do.

9.1 AI-Driven Threat Detection

AI-powered threat detection is similar to having a bodyguard for your digital life who is extremely intelligent and vigilant. It continuously scans, analyses, and forecasts the potential source of the next assault rather than passively waiting for something negative to happen. It searches through mounds of data, including system logs, network traffic, and user behaviour, using machine learning to identify patterns that shout "problem." Imagine it as a computerised Sherlock Holmes, solving puzzles that people might overlook. What's the best part? It becomes increasingly intelligent. Its ability to detect danger before it materialises improves with the number of threats it faces. Being ten steps ahead of hackers is more important than simply stopping them.

AI-driven threat detection protects your sanity as well as your bacon. Security teams are overloaded with alarms, let's face it. The majority of them are false alarms, but the one important alert can be hidden among all the others. AI clears the clutter by ranking risks according to their seriousness and providing security professionals with a clear path forward. It's similar to having a co-pilot who helps you direct the ship away from the iceberg in addition to warning you about it. AI is not merely a nice-to-have; it is a necessity in a world where cyberattacks are becoming more frequent, cunning, and devastating. It is cybersecurity's future, and that future has already here.

AI's introduction into cybersecurity has been nothing short of groundbreaking. AI-powered solutions prioritise intelligence and adaptability above static rules and signature-based detection, which are the mainstays of traditional security measures. Through the use of behavioural analytics, deep learning methods, and machine learning models, organisations may identify risks before they become real and react independently and with previously unheard-of accuracy.

AI plays a variety of roles in cybersecurity. By evaluating enormous datasets to detect possible breaches, it improves threat intelligence and predictive analytics. By using behavioural analysis, AI can identify typical user behaviour and highlight any differences that can point to insider threats or credential abuse. Without the need for human participation, automated incident response makes sure that harmful activity is stopped in real time, minimising damage. AI also plays a key role in identifying social engineering and deepfakes by carefully examining text, speech, and image content for manipulation. By eliminating false positives and giving priority to real threats, artificial intelligence (AI) streamlines processes even at Security Operations Centres (SOC), hence lowering analyst fatigue.

However, AI-driven cybersecurity has drawbacks in addition to benefits. The possibility of adversarial assaults, in which cybercriminals alter AI algorithms by introducing false data, is increasing. System reliability can be decreased by bias in AI training datasets, which can result in misclassifications and false positives. Concerns about privacy and regulatory compliance are also raised by AI's reliance on sensitive data. Many organisations continue to face obstacles due to the high cost and complexity of implementing AI-driven solutions. But as AI develops further, so will the strategies for resolving these issues, guaranteeing its position as a cornerstone of cybersecurity.

9.2 Blockchain-Based Security Solutions

Although blockchain technology is most famous for enabling cryptocurrency, its applications in cybersecurity are becoming more and more clear. Fundamentally, blockchain provides a tamper-proof, immutable ledger, which is a perfect feature for protecting transactions, guaranteeing data integrity, and decentralising identity management. Blockchain dramatically lowers the risks of data breaches and unauthorised access by removing central points of failure.

Blockchain has a significant impact on cybersecurity. Users can safely manage their digital identities via decentralised identity management, which goes beyond conventional, hacker-prone centralised databases. By avoiding unwanted changes, cryptographic hashing guarantees that data saved on the blockchain stays unchangeable. Smart contracts also automate security procedures, identifying and reacting to fraudulent activity in real time. Blockchain improves authenticity and transparency in supply networks, thwarting counterfeiting and guaranteeing product integrity. Decentralised networks that divide workloads among several nodes can lessen vulnerability to even the long-standing cyberthreat of Distributed Denial-of-Service (DDoS) assaults.

Blockchain is revolutionising cybersecurity and is more than just a trendy term. Imagine a world in which every digital identity, transaction, and piece of data is encrypted beyond cracking and dispersed throughout a network so large that it would be impossible to hack even a single grain of sand off a beach. That is blockchain's power. Making data *unhackable* is equally as important as making it secure. And that's a huge problem in a world when data breaches happen as frequently as coffee spills. Blockchain technology is subtly changing our understanding of trust in the digital era, from safeguarding financial transactions to preserving medical information.

Let's not mince words, though: blockchain is not a panacea. Although it still has some growing pains to get past, it does have the potential to make the internet a safer place. Because transaction processing times are still slower than in traditional databases, scalability problems still exist. Governments are still having difficulty defining precise frameworks for blockchain-based security, which contributes to regulatory ambiguity. Additionally, businesses frequently struggle to integrate legacy systems, which hinders their wider adoption. Vulnerabilities in smart contracts are arguably the biggest worry since improperly drafted contracts might create security gaps that allow for financial losses and exploitation. Notwithstanding these drawbacks, blockchain technology is only expected to grow in importance in cybersecurity, holding up the prospect of more durable, transparent, and verifiable digital security in the future.

It's not particularly user-friendly, to begin with. It can seem like an impossible task to integrate blockchain technology with current systems. Furthermore, in a rainstorm, blockchain transactions may be slower than a dial-up connection. The elephant in the room, smart contracts, should also not be overlooked. Although they are excellent in theory, they can become a hacker's paradise with only one small coding mistake. The difficulty is that all innovative technologies have initial issues. Just like the internet took time to develop, blockchain will also take time. As the kinks are worked out, blockchain has the potential to become the foundation of a more secure and open digital society. The potential is too great to ignore.

9.3 Case Study: IBM's AI-Driven Security in Action

IBM's threat prevention strategy is among the most impressive real-world examples of AI-driven cybersecurity. Leading the way in AI-integrated security, IBM has created cutting-edge solutions that identify and eliminate online threats before they have a chance to worsen. At the core of this strategy is IBM QRadar, an AI-powered Security Information and Event Management (SIEM) platform that revolutionizes how organizations defend against cyberattacks.

IBM QRadar uses machine learning models to identify irregularities and possible threats by continually monitoring network traffic, log files, and endpoint activity. While AI-driven incident prioritisation reduces alert fatigue by prioritising threats according to their severity, automated threat-hunting capabilities guarantee that cyber hazards are detected early. QRadar's capabilities are further enhanced by IBM's Watson AI, which offers deep cybersecurity insights gleaned from enormous datasets.

A real-world example is the greatest way to demonstrate IBM QRadar's impact. A sophisticated ransomware attack was launched against a Fortune 500 financial firm. Unusual login patterns and illegal encryption attempts were detected by QRadar's AI algorithms, which isolated compromised systems before the ransomware could propagate. This quick reaction prevented the business from suffering millions of dollars in possible damages, proving the enormous worth of AI-driven security.

9.4 Future-Proofing Your Cybersecurity Career

The truth is that developing an attitude of inquiry and adaptability is more important for future-proofing your cybersecurity job than just accumulating credentials or learning the newest technical terms. If you're not always learning, you're falling behind in the rapidly evolving field of cybersecurity. The good news is that you don't need to be an expert in every field. Rather, concentrate on developing into a problem-solver who is at ease navigating new technology and making quick decisions. The secret is to remain curious and never stop trying, whether you're working with Web3 projects, playing with AI technologies, or investigating the possibilities of blockchain technology. Additionally, share your journey rather than learning in isolation. Post about your work, start blogs, and interact with the cybersecurity community. By tackling real-world issues and showcasing your work, you're not only securing your professional future but also influencing the direction of cybersecurity as a whole.

In order to remain relevant, cybersecurity experts need to adjust as AI, blockchain, and Web3 reshape the field. The environment now requires knowledge of machine learning, decentralised security, and cryptographic protocols rather than just firewalls and antivirus software. Professionals in cybersecurity who adapt to these developments will be at the forefront of a demanding and fulfilling field.

To succeed in this changing field, people need to develop a wide range of skills. These days, AI and machine learning are essential to cybersecurity, especially for automated responses and threat detection. With smart contract audits, decentralised identity management, and cryptographic concepts constituting key knowledge areas, blockchain security expertise is becoming more and more valuable. The next generation of safe online interactions is also being shaped by Web3 technologies, such as zero-trust architectures and decentralised applications (dApps). Professionals should be proficient in DevSecOps and cloud security in addition to technical skills to provide strong protection for cloud-based infrastructures. Since penetration testing and red teaming are still essential elements of cybersecurity strategy, a thorough understanding of threat intelligence and ethical hacking is equally important. Finally, as regulatory frameworks are constantly changing in response to emerging threats, managing cybersecurity compliance and risk is crucial.

Continuous learning is necessary to stay ahead in the cybersecurity sector. Engaging in Capture The Flag (CTF) challenges, contributing to open-source security projects, and maintaining current certifications (CISSP, CEH, CISM, AWS Security) are all great ways to develop competence. Career prospects are further improved by attending conferences, networking with specialists in the field, and demonstrating practical experience on websites like LinkedIn and GitHub. To obtain a competitive edge, professionals must, above all, embrace emerging technologies and experiment with blockchain applications and AI-driven security tools.

9.5 Final Thoughts

The convergence of Web3, blockchain, and AI is shaping the future of cybersecurity. Blockchain offers new paradigms for securing identities and transactions, while AI-driven threat detection is revolutionising the way cyber risks are recognised and reduced. Professionals in cybersecurity must rise to the challenge as these technologies develop further, learning new techniques and adjusting to a constantly shifting threat scenario. A safer, more secure future will be shaped in large part by those who embrace innovation in the digital world, which is at a turning point.

Part III Cybersecurity Networking

Chapter 10: Building a Global Cybersecurity Network

Professionals in cybersecurity need to stay alert and connected in a constantly changing digital environment. Innovation, legislation, and ongoing threat adaptability shape the worldwide cybersecurity environment. Attending conferences and engaging in professional groups are crucial tactics for career advancement, skill development, and business prospects in order to stay abreast of these advances. The top cybersecurity groups and conferences that provide professionals with unmatched networking possibilities, technical insights, and career growth prospects are examined in this chapter.

10.1 Top Cybersecurity Conferences

Black Hat USA, which takes place in Las Vegas, is one of the most well-known cybersecurity conferences. Black Hat offers state-of-the-art research, vulnerabilities, and solutions and is well-known for its comprehensive technical training and insights from top industry figures. For practitioners, researchers, and executives looking to explore new trends and commercial prospects, it's a great place to network. One of the biggest and oldest hacker gatherings, DEF CON, takes place in Las Vegas and brings together government officials, security researchers, and ethical hackers. The event is a must-attend for cybersecurity aficionados who want to test their skills and get knowledge from practical demonstrations because it includes hands-on hacking camps, competitions, and debates on the newest cyber threats.

Enterprise security, governance, and risk management are the main topics of the San Francisco-hosted RSA Conference. Top executives, suppliers, and legislators are drawn to it to talk about how to reduce cyber dangers. RSA is essential for people interested in enterprise-level solutions and cybersecurity business strategies. The Tel Aviv-based Cybertech Global, on the other hand, offers a venue for cybersecurity entrepreneurs, investors, and companies to work together on cutting-edge security solutions, which makes it perfect for anyone looking to cooperate on a company or explore investment prospects.

The Gartner Security & Risk Management Summit, which brings together industry professionals to discuss data privacy, threat intelligence, and resilience strategies, is a great place to go if you're looking for insights into risk management, AI-driven cybersecurity, and governance. Gartner's research-based insights on industry trends are useful to executives and security strategists. The Forum of Incident Response and Security Teams (FIRST) is hosting the FIRST Conference, which focusses on international cybersecurity collaboration and the exchange of threat intelligence. For security professionals working in threat mitigation and incident response jobs, it is especially helpful.

European cybersecurity experts can attend London's Infosecurity Europe. This conference offers a great chance to interact with European security vendors and regulatory agencies through a combination of technical workshops, business networking sessions, and thought leadership panels. The International Ethical Hacking Conference (eHaCON) in Kolkata, India, is another unique event. A 12-hour hackathon (Dcyfr), a three-minute scholarly thesis presentation (3MST), and ethical hacking workshops, cryptography, and steganography challenges are all part of eHaCON. It is the first of its kind to mix AI, cybersecurity, and law in academia and industry, and it also include industry meetings, panel discussions, keynote addresses, and technical sessions.

10.2 Key Cybersecurity Communities

The best way to advance your profession and keep ahead of the curve is to join important cybersecurity communities. These communities provide a wealth of information, opportunity, and teamwork, whether it's Reddit's r/cybersecurity, Twitter's #Infosec community, or specialised forums like Hack The Box and Stack Overflow. Beyond conferences, participating in other groups can be beneficial for cybersecurity workers. Professionals in cybersecurity and IT governance can obtain certifications, training, and networking opportunities from ISACA (Information Systems Audit and Control Association). In addition to offering a global network of security experts for forums, mentoring, and information exchange, the CISSP certification is administered by the International Information System Security Certification Consortium (ISC)².

The Open Web Application Security Project, or OWASP, is a nonprofit that offers security best practices and resources for anyone interested in application security. Likewise, through its alumni clubs, the SANS Institute Alumni & Community provides networking opportunities in addition to practical cybersecurity training and certifications. HackerOne and Bugcrowd are platforms that link ethical hackers with companies for vulnerability disclosure projects and bug bounty programs. Professionals interested in ethical hacking can join these platforms. Professionals can also keep updated and network with industry leaders by participating in cybersecurity discussions on social media sites like LinkedIn and Twitter.

The sense of community is delivered right to your door by local chapters of International Information Systems Security Certification Consortium (ISC)2 or DEF CON organisations. Instead of only lurking, get active. Contribute to projects, ask questions, and share your thoughts. These communities are about more than simply education; they're about forming connections with potential mentors, partners, and even employers. Your network is your greatest asset in cybersecurity, and these networks are where you'll meet like-minded individuals.

10.3 Case Study: How Attending One Conference Led to a $100K Consulting Gig

John, a seasoned cybersecurity analyst, had always been passionate about security research but had never actively engaged in the global cybersecurity community. Despite his work involving threat mitigation and enterprise network security, he felt that his career was stagnating. He made the decision to go to Black Hat USA in order to investigate fresh prospects after being encouraged by a mentor. John met a cybersecurity executive at a networking event at the conference and participated in courses on advanced penetration testing. John offered his work-related ideas with them as they talked about industry trends. The executive was impressed by his knowledge and asked whether John had thought about consulting.

John followed up with a LinkedIn connection after exchanging contact information. A week later, he got a message regarding a possible consulting job for a security-challenged fintech business. John was asked to perform a preliminary security evaluation, and he gave a presentation of his results along with a plan for improving their security posture. Because of his experience, he was awarded a $100,000 six-month consulting contract that included staff training, security policy creation, and penetration testing.

John's experience brings to light a number of important lessons. A simple discussion at a convention resulted in a lucrative opportunity, demonstrating the importance of networking. Follow-up is important; his proactive communication style made an introduction into a business transaction. Expertise is essential; sharing knowledge and exhibiting abilities can lead to unexpected opportunities.

John's tale is about being there and prepared to take advantage of the opportunity, not only about chance. Although, let's face it, the free stuff is a nice perk, attending conferences like Black Hat is about more than just listening to presentations. They involve placing oneself in the space where it takes place. Attending workshops wasn't enough for John; he also needed to participate, ask questions, and share his personal experiences. That's what set him apart. He wasn't just chatting business when he started that conversation with the executive; he was also demonstrating his abilities. And that's the key: expertise combined with confidence.

John continued after the meeting. He didn't merely gather business cards and cross his fingers. He made sure they remembered him, followed up, and remained in their sights. That is the strength of initiative. And he didn't just turn up when the chance presented itself; he showed it off. His first evaluation was a master class in problem-solving, not merely a report. He provided remedies in addition to pointing out shortcomings. A one-time engagement became a six-month contract because of that. What's the lesson here? Opportunities don't just come your way; you have to make them by being ready, tenacious, and demonstrating your value. Be more than simply a face in the throng the next time you're at a conference. Be the one who people remember.

10.4 Actionable Takeaway: Leveraging Networking to Land Global Opportunities

Let's face it, networking is more than merely tactfully passing out business cards at conferences or amassing LinkedIn connections. It's about establishing connections that lead to opportunities you were unaware of. Your network is your net worth in the realm of cybersecurity. Consider this: not just what you know, but who you know can lead to some of the best initiatives, employment, and partnerships. Don't be afraid to take risks. Participate in forums, join online communities, and don't be afraid to send direct messages with queries or thoughts. Whether it's getting invited to work on a cutting-edge project or securing a remote employment with a multinational corporation, the more you connect, the more you'll find yourself in the right place at the right moment.

Building a network is a two-way street. It's about what you can give, not just what you can get. Offer assistance, share your expertise, and show real interest in what other people are doing. People remember you when you contribute value to your network. Additionally, they will consider you first when chances arise. Furthermore, networking need not be daunting or formal. It can be as easy as leaving a comment on a piece that speaks to you, working together on an open-source project, or simply striking up a conversation after a webinar. The bottom line? You could initiate a discussion today that leads to your next big break. Therefore, go out there and create opportunities instead of waiting for them to find you.

Professionals should begin by determining which conferences and forums best suit their interests and areas of expertise in order to get the most out of cybersecurity communities and conferences. The likelihood of making beneficial connections is increased by giving priority to conferences that draw decision-makers and leaders in the sector. Making a strong personal pitch, studying speakers and attendees in advance, and updating LinkedIn profiles with the most recent work and experience are all ways to improve networking effectiveness.

Professionals should actively participate in networking events and workshops, share their knowledge, and demonstrate genuine interest in the work of others in order to have meaningful interactions once they arrive at the event. Making connections on LinkedIn and exchanging contact information guarantees that these connections last after the conference. Staying in touch and following up are equally crucial; offering collaboration chances, sharing pertinent industry information, and sending a message within a few days of meeting someone can help cement new relationships.

Developing a personal brand also improves employment prospects. Professionals in the cybersecurity industry can differentiate themselves by giving talks, producing articles, taking part in panel discussions, working on open-source projects, and gaining specialised knowledge. Like John, professionals can access possibilities that define their careers by skilfully utilising cybersecurity conferences and groups. Making connections is only one aspect of networking; another is developing deep connections that spur development, creativity, and achievement.

10.5 Final Thoughts

Creating a worldwide cybersecurity network involves more than just going to events or participating in online forums; it also entails actively participating, exchanging expertise, and cultivating deep connections that promote career development and industry advancement. Maintaining relationships with peers, thought leaders, and experts is crucial as the cybersecurity landscape changes in order to learn about new threats, cutting-edge technologies, and best practices. By investing in networking and cooperation, cybersecurity professionals can access new possibilities, career advancements, and creative solutions that will influence the field's future, whether through conferences, professional groups, or digital platforms.

Chapter 11: Building a Cybersecurity Side Hustle

Allow me to assist you in generating passive money from your expertise in cybersecurity!

The need for specialists is greater than ever as the cybersecurity sector grows. The interesting news is that you don't have to work a typical 9–5 job if you have cybersecurity expertise. There are several methods to make your expertise into a lucrative side business that will help people and companies stay secure online while also generating passive revenue. Consider earning money while you sleep by using software tools, blogs, YouTube videos, online courses, or even consultancy. Does it sound too good to be real? It isn't. Many cybersecurity experts have already accomplished this, and we'll go over how you can achieve it in this chapter. We'll also go deeply into the tale of Alex, a YouTuber who specialises in cybersecurity and made a million-dollar business out of his hobby.

11.1 Making Money with Cybersecurity: What Are Your Options?

Blogging and Content Writing: Turning Words into Wealth

Starting a blog can be your path to success if you enjoy writing and have a talent for simplifying difficult cybersecurity subjects. By writing about cybersecurity regulations, penetration testing, ethical hacking, or personal digital security, many experts establish their expertise in the sector. After your site becomes popular, you can make money via sponsorships, affiliate marketing, and Google AdSense. The secret is to choose an area of interest, optimise your website for search engines, and share your content on forums for cybersecurity and social media. You can earn more money if you increase the amount of traffic to your website.

YouTube and Online Courses: Teaching and Earning

On YouTube, cybersecurity is one of the most popular subjects. People are keen to learn about security technologies, hacking methods, and safeguarding their online identities. Making video content could be revolutionary if you feel at ease speaking in front of a camera. Start by deciding on a content format that works for you, such as product reviews, news analysis, live hacking demonstrations, or lessons. You may start making money with YouTube adverts, sponsorships, and even selling your own online courses on sites like Teachable or Udemy if you have a nice video and edit it well.

Cybersecurity Consulting and Freelancing: Getting Paid for Your Expertise

Not everyone has the time or means to create a YouTube channel or blog. However, you can begin earning money very immediately through consulting if you already have cybersecurity knowledge. Penetration testing, security audits, and compliance assessments are essential for businesses, particularly small ones, but they frequently lack the funds for a full-time specialist. All you need is a profile on freelance marketplaces like Upwork, Fiverr, or Toptal, as well as a solid portfolio that highlights your abilities. To draw consumers, you can initially provide complimentary consultations. You can market other services like security training and continuous risk monitoring after you've established yourself.

Creating Cybersecurity Tools and Software: Solving Problems, Making Profits

If development is your field of expertise, think about creating cybersecurity tools. A freemium business model, which offers a basic version for free while charging for premium services, can be used to make money from simple goods like password managers, network scanners, or phishing detection systems. Find a typical cybersecurity issue that can be automated first. Create a Minimum Viable Product (MVP), test it among cybersecurity experts, then advertise it at cybersecurity conferences and tech forums. You can make your tool a full-fledged business if it becomes popular.

Writing Cybersecurity eBooks: Sharing Knowledge, Earning Royalties

For some professionals, creating books is more important than blogging. An eBook can be a great way to make extra money if you are well-versed in subjects like secure coding, GDPR compliance, or ethical hacking. The steps are straightforward: pick a popular subject, write about it in an interesting and useful way, and then sell it on websites like Gumroad, Amazon Kindle, or even your own. Use mailing lists, cybersecurity blogs, and LinkedIn to promote your book and increase sales.

Running a Paid Cybersecurity Newsletter: Getting Paid for Exclusive Insights

You may provide a loyal subscriber base with premium cybersecurity information using systems like Substack and Ghost. For in-depth security updates, unique research reports, and professional viewpoints on new cyberthreats, readers are prepared to pay. Choose a niche, such as virus analysis, privacy regulations, or dark web intelligence, and then produce a combination of free and commercial content to achieve success. Use social media to spread the word, collaborate with cybersecurity influencers, and expand your audience through networking and guest posts.

11.2 Case Study: How a Cybersecurity YouTuber Built a $1M Business

Let me introduce you to Alex, a normal guy who has a love for cybersecurity and a talent for simplifying difficult subjects so that everyone can grasp them. He launched a YouTube channel because he loved teaching, not because he hoped to become famous or wealthy. His security awareness and ethical hacking videos were interesting, easy to follow, and full of useful advice. Thousands of people were signing up before he realised it. What started off as a pastime swiftly grew into something much more. Alex became astute at making money off of his channel as his following expanded. He created an entire ecosystem rather than depending simply on one source of income. Ad income was the first. He began making money from those YouTube advertisements after he reached 10,000 subscribers. Sponsorships followed. Because they knew his audience believed him, cybersecurity companies flocked to him to pay for product reviews. Alex didn't stop there, though. In order to meet the increasing demand for cybersecurity education, he developed beginner-friendly online courses on sites like Teachable and Udemy. In addition, he experimented with affiliate marketing, recommending tools and receiving payments. Additionally, companies began contacting him for consultancy assignments as his reputation increased.

The worst part is that Alex didn't just relax and take pleasure in the money coming in. He put his profits back into new content, promotion, and better equipment. He started a paid cybersecurity newsletter and ventured into eBooks. What began as a side project grew into a multimillion-dollar enterprise in just three years. Alex demonstrated that you can transform a YouTube channel into a career that changes lives by quitting his day job and focussing entirely on cybersecurity. His narrative serves as a guide for anyone hoping to transform their area of expertise into a successful business, in addition to being inspirational. What is preventing you from following suit, then?

Alex's tale demonstrates that you don't need a fancy title or a corporate job to succeed in cybersecurity; it's not some distant, unachievable fantasy. All you need is a little imagination, a lot of hard work, and the guts to take risks. Perhaps you're sitting on a wealth of information at the moment and wondering, "Who's going to care what I have to say?" I promise that someone will. The field of cybersecurity is in dire need of someone who can make sense of the complex concepts. There is room for you to establish your own niche, whether it is through YouTube, blogs, courses, or consultancy. So don't wait for approval. Begin producing, sharing, and constructing. One blog post, one video, or one chat could lead to your big idea. Are you prepared to take the initial step? That's the only question.

11.3 How to Start Your Own Cybersecurity Side Hustle: A Roadmap

Creating your own cybersecurity side business is about more than just earning additional money; it's about transforming your passion into a source of income and your abilities into a brand. You don't have to quit your day job or have a brilliant concept to get started, though. All you need is the courage to take risks and a well-defined plan. Let's dissect it.

Choose your business model and niche first. Being an expert in one area is more important than being a jack-of-all-trades. Do penetration tests come naturally to you? Are compliance frameworks your thing? Or perhaps you have a talent for simplifying difficult security ideas into manageable chunks. Own it, whatever it is. Next, consider how you wish to make money off of it. Perhaps you launch a blog, develop online courses, or provide independent consultancy. The secret is to match your abilities with a scalable and genuine business concept.

Next, create a presence on the internet that shouts "expert." It is imperative to have a sleek website, an impressive LinkedIn profile, and active participation in cybersecurity communities. This is about being discoverable, not simply about seeming professional. You want your name to appear when someone searches for "cybersecurity expert" on Google. Begin producing material that highlights your areas of expertise. Regardless of the format you use—blog entries, YouTube videos, eBooks—make sure to provide value. Not only does excellent content increase credibility, but it also increases trust. And faith? That's how followers become clients.

It's time to start making money once you've got things going. Promote affiliate products, sell courses, offer freelance services, or apply for YouTube advertisements. You may experiment until you find what suits you best, which is the great thing about side hustles. Additionally, don't be scared to scale and automate as business expand. Utilise technologies to do the tedious labour, such as scheduling social media posts, email marketing, and even engaging independent contractors to do graphic design or video editing. Freeing up time to concentrate on the big picture is the aim.

Lastly, because it is essential, network like your side business depends on it. Collaborate with others in the business, publish guest posts, speak at events, and partner with influencers. Your side business will expand more quickly the more connections you make. Keep in mind that developing a reputation is equally as important as developing a business. Additionally, your reputation is crucial in the field of cybersecurity. What're you waiting for, then? Your side business is out there, just waiting for you to seize it. Go ahead and make it happen.

11.4 Final Thoughts: Your Cybersecurity Side Hustle Starts Now

The need in the cybersecurity sector is limitless, which is its beauty. Your knowledge can help people and businesses stay safe while producing steady revenue with the correct approach. Whether you're starting a blog, launching a YouTube channel, building security tools, or offering consulting services, there's a path for you. Success won't happen overnight, but with consistency, smart monetization, and strategic networking, your cybersecurity side hustle could eventually replace your full-time job. And who knows? Maybe your story will be the next million-dollar success case.

Chapter 12: Your Cybersecurity Success Blueprint

The world of cybersecurity is a battlefield—one where the threats never stop evolving and the professionals defending against them must constantly sharpen their skills. The career opportunities are vast, but many stumble into traps that slow their progress or even push them out of the industry.

Some fall into the false comfort of their certifications, thinking a CISSP or CEH will carry them for life. Others focus so much on mastering the technical side that they forget the importance of communication, networking, or personal branding. And then there are those who simply stop learning, assuming what worked yesterday will work tomorrow.

Cybersecurity isn't just a job—it's a mindset. It's about being the person who sees the cracks in the system before they become gaping holes. But here's the catch: you can't just rely on what you know today. The game changes fast, and if you're not constantly learning, you're already falling behind. That means staying curious, experimenting with new tools, and diving into areas that scare you a little. The best cybersecurity pros aren't just experts; they're lifelong students. Therefore, consider whether you are learning or simply coasting.

Being skilled at your work isn't enough in a subject as cutthroat as cybersecurity; you also need to be noticed. This entails creating a personal brand that exudes legitimacy. You can launch a YouTube channel, write blogs, speak at events, or share your expertise on LinkedIn. Opportunities come to you rather than the other way around when you are perceived as a thought leader. The worst part is that it's not about flaunting. The goal is to add value. You will receive more in return for your contributions. Put yourself out there instead of hiding behind your keyboard.

Remember the importance of relationships as well. Cybersecurity is a team sport, not an individual one. Making relationships can lead to opportunities you were unaware existed. Participate in online forums, go to conferences, and don't be scared to approach people you respect. Your ideal employment, a partnership, or even a mentoring could result from a simple conversation. The problem is that networking is about giving as much as it is about receiving. Provide assistance, impart knowledge, and be a someone that people want to collaborate with. By developing sincere connections, you're not just furthering your career but also influencing the direction of the sector. What're you waiting for, then?

You must change the way you think if you want to succeed in cybersecurity. You must have a plan. Go make your mark.

12.1. The Career-Killing Mistakes You Must Avoid
Mistake #1: Thinking Learning Stops After a Certification

What is the biggest mistake cybersecurity professionals make? Thinking they've "made it" after passing a few exams. Sure, getting a certification is an achievement, but the digital threat landscape changes too fast for a framed certificate to keep you safe. Hackers innovate. New vulnerabilities emerge. Staying relevant requires relentless curiosity. The real pros are the ones who never stop learning. They're the ones reading security blogs over breakfast, tinkering with new tools in their home labs, and jumping into Capture the Flag (CTF) challenges just for fun. They're always one step ahead—because they know in cybersecurity, standing still is the same as falling behind.

Here's the hard truth: getting a certification like CISSP or CEH is just the beginning, not the finish line. Too many people treat certifications like a golden ticket, thinking once they've got that piece of paper, they're set for life. But here's the reality: cybersecurity doesn't stand still. New threats pop up every day, and the tools and tactics you learned last year might already be outdated. Certifications are great for opening doors, but they won't keep you in the room. If you want to stay relevant, you've got to keep learning—whether it's diving into the latest hacking techniques, experimenting with new tools, or staying on top of industry trends. The moment you stop learning is the moment you start falling behind. So, don't let that certification collect dust. Use it as a launchpad, not a landing spot. Keep pushing, keep growing, and keep proving you're not just certified—you're capable.

Mistake #2: Ignoring Soft Skills

You might be the best ethical hacker in the room, but if you can't explain a security risk to a CEO in plain English, your impact will be limited. Technical brilliance alone won't get you a leadership role, a high-paying consulting gig, or a shot at the top security jobs. Cybersecurity is as much about storytelling as it is about scripts and firewalls. Can you write a security report that a non-technical manager can actually understand? Can you present your findings in a way that convinces a boardroom to take action? The best in the industry isn't just tech-savvy—they're effective communicators.

In cybersecurity, technical skills might get you in the door, but soft skills are what keep you in the building. You could be the best hacker or the most brilliant coder in the room, but if you can't explain a vulnerability to a non-technical CEO or work well with a team during a high-pressure breach, you're going to hit a ceiling. Communication, collaboration, and problem-solving are just as critical as knowing how to patch a server or analyze malware. Think about it—cybersecurity isn't just about machines; it's about people. You've got to be able to build trust, influence decisions, and sometimes even calm nerves during a crisis. So, don't just focus on mastering Python or Kali Linux. Hone your ability to tell a story, lead a meeting, or negotiate like a pro. Because at the end of the day, the best cybersecurity pros aren't just tech wizards—they're trusted advisors who can bridge the gap between the technical and the human side of the business.

Mistake #3: Believing Certifications Alone Guarantee Success

Let's be real—certifications look great on paper, but they're not a magic ticket to success. Sure, they'll help you get your foot in the door, but once you're inside, no one cares how many letters follow your name if you can't deliver where it counts. Employers aren't just checking boxes; they're looking for people who can actually do the work. Think about it: Would you rather hire someone who aced a test or someone who's rolled up their sleeves, messed around in a home lab, and fixed real problems? Exactly. Certifications teach you the rules, but experience teaches you how to play the game—and win.

So, how do you bridge the gap between theory and action? Get your hands dirty. Set up a home lab and break things on purpose (ethically, of course). Jump into open-source projects—nothing proves your skills like code that real people use. Or try bug bounty hunting, where you test your hacking chops against actual systems and get paid for it. These aren't just resume boosters; they're proof that you can think on your feet and solve problems when it matters. At the end of the day, a wall of certificates might impress your mom, but real-world experience? That's what lands the job—and keeps you thriving in it.

Mistake #4: Trying to Be a Generalist

Let's face it—cybersecurity is a beast. It's got more branches than a rainforest: penetration testing, digital forensics, incident response, risk management, compliance, cloud security… the list never ends. And here's the hard truth: trying to learn it all is like trying to become fluent in every language on the planet. Spoiler alert—you'll burn out before you even get close. The real pros don't try to do everything; they pick their lane and own it. Want to be the Sherlock Holmes of threat intelligence? Go all in on that. Obsessed with locking down cloud environments? Dive deep into AWS and Azure security. Mastery beats mediocrity every time.

Here's the secret: specialization is your superpower. Companies don't need jacks-of-all-trades—they need experts who can solve their toughest problems. When you focus, you stop being just another IT person and become the person—the one everyone calls when things get real. So, pick your passion, drill down, and build your reputation as the go-to guru in your field. Because in cybersecurity, depth wins over breadth every single time.

Mistake #5: Underestimating the Power of Networking

Here's the inside scoop—some of the hottest cybersecurity gigs never even make it to job boards. They are acquired through traditional networking, word-of-mouth, and referrals. The issue is that too many professionals are cooped up behind their laptops, working alone, while the greatest chances pass them by. Do you want to advance? Put yourself out there now. Attend trade shows, participate in online discussion boards, and use blogs or social media to offer your expertise. Hiring managers and influencers may see your impressive LinkedIn profile or a few witty tweets before a position is even formally posted.

Consider networking to be your covert tool. Technical proficiency is only one aspect of cybersecurity; other factors include reputation, trust, and being at the forefront of people's minds when chances arise. The more you interact with the community, the more doors will open for you without you having to knock. Create a blog article that addresses a prevalent issue, leave a thoughtful remark on a thought leader's piece, or simply go out for coffee with someone in your industry. Connections become referrals, and referrals become employment opportunities. In this field, connections help you win, but talent only gets you into the game.

12.2 How to Stay Ahead in This Ever-Changing Industry
In cybersecurity, being proactive is more important than simply avoiding errors. The best professionals don't wait for opportunities; they create them. Here's how you stay ahead.

Always Be Learning
Cybercriminals aren't slowing down, and neither should you. Stay informed about the latest threats by following security blogs like *Krebs on Security*, *Dark Reading*, and *Threatpost*. Join cybersecurity Slack groups

and forums where professionals discuss new attack techniques in real-time. The more you know, the better equipped you are.

Build a Home Lab and Experiment

Nothing beats hands-on practice. Set up a virtual lab where you can safely test penetration testing tools, analyze malware, and simulate attacks. Experiment with Metasploit, Burp Suite, and other security tools. The more you play, the sharper your skills will become.

Understand AI and Automation

AI is reshaping cybersecurity. Machine learning is being used to detect anomalies, automate threat responses, and even predict attacks before they happen. If you're not learning how AI impacts security, you risk being left behind. Dive into Python automation, explore SIEM tools, and understand how AI-driven threat detection works. It's the future.

Engage with the Community

Cybersecurity isn't a solo sport. The best in the industry contribute to open-source security projects, mentor newcomers, and volunteer for cybersecurity awareness initiatives. The more you give back, the more you learn—and the more you get noticed.

12.3 Your 90-Day Roadmap to Cybersecurity Success

You've got the knowledge—now it's time to execute. Follow this structured plan, and in three months, you'll be on a fast track to cybersecurity success.

Phase 1: Building Your Foundation (Days 1–30)

Start with the basics. Choose a cybersecurity specialization. Enroll in an online course through Coursera, Cybrary, or TryHackMe. Set up a home lab and begin experimenting. Read security blogs daily. Join a cybersecurity community like OWASP or ISC2. Most importantly, start a personal cybersecurity project—something that lets you apply what you're learning in a real way.

Phase 2: Hands-On Experience (Days 31–60)

Now it's time to get practical. Join a Capture the Flag (CTF) challenge. Start a cybersecurity blog or LinkedIn series to share what you're learning. Network with industry professionals. Sign up for a certification course, but don't just study—apply the knowledge. Try your hand at bug bounty programs. Attend at least one cybersecurity webinar or conference to gain insights from experts.

Phase 3: Career Acceleration (Days 61–90)

This is where you start making cybersecurity work for you. Apply for freelance security gigs. Launch a YouTube channel or podcast to educate others. Contribute to open-source projects. Polish your resume and LinkedIn profile to highlight your hands-on experience. Prepare for cybersecurity job interviews by practicing common technical and behavioural questions. If you're feeling confident, start pitching your cybersecurity consulting services to small businesses.

12.4 The Blueprint is Yours—Now Take Action

A thriving cybersecurity career doesn't happen by accident. It's built step by step—through continuous learning, practical experience, strategic networking, and a proactive mindset.

This roadmap is your guide, but the execution is on you. The best time to start was yesterday.

The next best time? Right now.

Your future in cybersecurity is waiting. Go seize it.

Conclusion

The Cybersecurity Mastery Manifesto

"Cybersecurity is much more than a matter of IT." — Stephane Nappo

You've made it to the concluding chapter, and that in itself is a testament to your commitment to mastering cybersecurity. Through the pages of this book, we've explored the fundamentals, dissected the most pressing threats, and mapped out a clear blueprint for building a thriving career in one of the world's most dynamic and critical industries. But reading is only half the battle—execution is what sets apart the dreamers from the achievers. Cybersecurity isn't just a profession; it's a mindset. It's about being persistent in the chase of knowledge, positive at times of budding intimidations, and calculated in building your career. It's about thoughtful that security is never absolute, but an incessant quest of resilience. This concluding chapter collates the whole thing together. We'll re-enter the most significant instructions, deliver crucial takeaways, and most significantly, issue a call to action. Your journey isn't finishing now—it's just the commencement.

Lessons That Will Shape Your Cybersecurity Journey

Every chapter in this book has been a stepping stone toward your cybersecurity success. Let's reflect on the essential lessons you've gained and how they will serve you in the real world.

The Cybersecurity Landscape is Constantly Evolving. The threats of today won't be the threats of tomorrow. Hackers innovate just as fast—if not faster—than defenders. We started this journey by exploring the landscape of cyber threats: ransomware, phishing, AI-driven attacks, and state-sponsored cyber warfare. Never get complacent. Keep your skills sharp, stay informed, and embrace the evolution of cybersecurity as an opportunity to grow.

"Change is the end result of all true learning." — Leo Buscaglia

Mastering Fundamentals is Non-Negotiable. You can't build a strong cybersecurity career on shaky foundations. Understanding network security, cryptography, risk management, and ethical hacking is critical. Without these fundamentals, even the most advanced tools and certifications will mean little. Master the basics before chasing advanced concepts. Your expertise should be deep, not just broad.

Cybersecurity is About Mindset, Not Just Tools. Yes, technical skills matter. But cybersecurity is a way of thinking—anticipating threats, recognizing weaknesses, and approaching security holistically. Whether you're an ethical hacker, risk manager, or security consultant, your ability to think like an attacker will define your success. Develop an attacker's mindset to become an effective defender.

"Amateurs hack systems, professionals hack people." — Bruce Schneier

Certifications Open Doors, but Skills Keep Them Open. You've learned about key certifications: CISSP, CEH, OSCP, Security+, and more. They prove credibility, but they don't replace real-world experience. Use certifications as stepping stones, not as the ultimate goal. Employers value practical experience over just credentials.

Specialization is the Fastest Path to Success. Cybersecurity is vast—penetration testing, incident response, cloud security, digital forensics, governance, and compliance. Generalists struggle to stand out. Specialists, on the other hand, command higher salaries and greater career opportunities. Find your niche. Become the go-to expert in one area rather than being average in many.

Your Network is Your Net Worth. The power of networking cannot be overstated. The best opportunities don't always come from job portals—they come from conversations, industry events, and personal connections. You've learned the importance of attending cybersecurity conferences, engaging on LinkedIn, and contributing to the community. Build relationships. A strong network can open doors that skills alone cannot.

"Surround yourself with those who are only going to lift you higher." — Oprah Winfrey

Continuous Learning is the Key to Staying Relevant. What worked yesterday won't necessarily work tomorrow. The best cybersecurity professionals are lifelong learners—constantly experimenting, testing, and adapting. Stay curious. Make learning a daily habit, not an occasional event.

Key Takeaways: The Cybersecurity Success Formula

To truly crush it in cybersecurity, you need a game plan—a success formula that turns knowledge into action and ambition into results. Start by mastering the fundamentals: get comfortable with networking, cryptography, and core security principles—they're the building blocks of everything else. But don't stop there; adopt an attacker's mindset. Learn to think like a hacker because the best defenders are the ones who can anticipate the next move. Then, roll up your sleeves and gain hands-on experience. Set up a home lab, dive into Capture the Flag (CTF) competitions, and contribute to open-source projects. Theory is great, but real skills are forged in the fire of practice. Stay ahead of the curve by keeping up with cybersecurity news, researching emerging threats, and continuously upskilling—this field doesn't stand still, and neither should you. Certifications? Sure, they help open doors, but skills are what keep you in the room. Focus on building real-world expertise that speaks louder than any piece of paper. Find your specialization and own it—whether it's ethical hacking, cloud security, digital forensics, or something else, become the go-to expert in your niche. And don't forget to network relentlessly. Engage with industry leaders, attend conferences, and be active in online communities—your network is your net worth in this game. Lastly, adopt a lifelong learning. Cybersecurity is a battleground that's always growing, and remaining updated isn't just a proposition; it's a prerequisite. Follow this recipe, and you're not just crafting a career, you're etching your name in history.

Your Call to Action: Own Your Cybersecurity Future

Reading this book has given you the knowledge, strategies, and roadmap to build an exceptional cybersecurity career. But knowledge without action is meaningless. Now, it's time for you to step up and take control of your journey.

Set Your 90-Day Action Plan. Here's the deal: momentum isn't something you wait for—it's something you create. And the best way to kickstart it? Set short-term, actionable goals that push you forward. Over the next 90 days, commit to picking your cybersecurity specialization—whether it's ethical hacking, cloud security, or digital forensics, find your niche and own it. Then, get your hands dirty in a lab. Theory is great, but nothing beats real-world experience. While you're at it, start building your network. Reach out to at least 10 industry pros—connect on LinkedIn, join a forum, or slide into a Twitter thread. Share your journey by writing a blog post or dropping some insights on LinkedIn. Not only does this show you're active, but it also positions you as someone who knows their stuff. And finally, level up your credentials by prepping for or earning a new certification. Whether it's CEH, CISSP, or something else, it's a game-changer for your resume. Ninety days might not sound like much, but with focus and hustle, it's enough to set your career on fire. Ready to make it happen? Let's go.

Join the Cybersecurity Community. Cybersecurity isn't a solo mission— it's a team sport. The best in the business don't just lock themselves in a room and hack away; they share knowledge, swap stories, and learn from each other. Think about it: the more you connect with others, the faster you grow. Start by diving into LinkedIn groups and Twitter threads where the cybersecurity community is buzzing. These are goldmines for real-time insights, debates, and opportunities. Don't stop there—get involved in forums like OWASP, ISC2, or Bugcrowd. These platforms aren't just about asking questions; they're about contributing, collaborating, and building your reputation as someone who knows their stuff. And here's a challenge for you: commit to attending at least one cybersecurity conference in the next six months. Whether it's Black Hat, DEF CON, or a local meetup, these events are where the magic happens. You'll encounter guides, learn innovative tools, and maybe even land your next big opening. Reminisce, your network is your net value in this area. So, get out there, start connecting, and watch how far you can go when you're not going it alone.

Never Settle for Mediocrity. The harsh reality is that being average in cybersecurity is a one-way ticket to irrelevance, not merely boring. There is no need for additional people in the world who simply play it safe and abide by the regulations. It needs leaders that aren't scared to make changes, innovators, and problem-solvers. This has nothing to do with learning textbooks or earning credentials; It involves getting your hands dirty, navigating the mess, and developing meaningful answers. You possess the abilities, the motivation, and the chance to create a profession that transforms the industry rather than merely making ends meet. The problem is that without taking that initial step, none of it will occur. What will it be, then? Are you prepared to start leaving your mark and stop observing from the sidelines? The digital world is waiting, and the clock is running out. Let's go.

"Success is not final; failure is not fatal: it is the courage to continue that counts." — Winston Churchill

Final Words: This is Just the Beginning

Cybersecurity is a calling, not simply a job. It's a field with enormous stakes, countless obstacles, and plenty of opportunities. Only those who are brave enough to seize them will find them everywhere. The world will always need individuals like you—the thinkers, the problem-solvers, the defenders—even while the threats and technology will continue to change. You're safeguarding the digital foundation of our world, not just repairing bugs or updating systems. What're you waiting for, then? Break down some boundaries by going out there. Create something durable. Be a strong barrier against the anarchy of the internet. Your trip is already underway; it is not just getting started. Are you prepared to be its owner? Let's go.

"The future belongs to those who prepare for it today." — Malcolm X

www.ingramcontent.com/pod-product-compliance
Lightning Source LLC
LaVergne TN
LVHW081528050326
832903LV00025B/1690